KU-394-514

Secret Ingredient

George Henry Fletcher (1878–1958)

George Fletcher (1904–73)

Paul Fletcher (1934–)

The three Fletcher generations

SECRET INGREDIENT

The Story of FLETCHERS' Seven Bakeries

by

Howard Hill

Published for Fletchers' Bakeries Ltd
by EP Publishing Ltd

Picture Credits
Dr Barry Biggs, Eaton Hall College of Education (p. 4).
Mary Evans Picture Library (p. 5).
Firth Brown Ltd (p. 11).
Sheffield City Libraries (p. 13).
Radio Times Hulton Picture Library (p. 18).
Graham Millson (front cover, p. 28).
Daily Mirror (p. 57).
Baker Perkins Holdings Ltd (pp. 75 and 79).
Sheffield Newspapers Ltd (pp. 71 and 83).
John Stonex (p. 88).
Fred Scatley (p. 89).

ISBN 0 7158 1263 7

First published in Great Britain 1978 for Fletchers' Bakeries Ltd, Claywheels Lane, Wadsley Bridge, Sheffield S6 1LY by EP Publishing Limited, Bradford Road, East Ardsley, Wakefield, West Yorkshire WF3 2JN.

Photoset, printed and bound
in Great Britain by
Redwood Burn Limited
Trowbridge & Esher

Acknowledgements

This book could not have been written without the assistance of many people who have willingly recalled their experiences upon which this history is based.

In the course of researching the material I have visited many business associates, representatives of firms which over the years have supplied Fletchers with the ingredients of the trade, food inspectors, customers, trade union officials, but above all those who have been employed in the different Fletcher bakehouses. All of them, some retired, have written and spoken freely of their impressions.

My special thanks are due to those who helped me to understand the skills of baking of which, before writing this book, I was totally ignorant. It is invidious to single out individuals but I must in this connection mention Mr Bert Slack and Mr Paul Fletcher.

I would also like to thank the staff of the Sheffield Central Library who willingly met all my requests for material; also the Denman Library of Retford and the Eaton Hall College of Education, Retford, both of which assisted in obtaining material about the early days of George Henry Fletcher.

It would be remiss of me not to mention *Leaven of Life*, an account of George Henry Fletcher's outstanding contribution to Sheffield's Labour Movement. I found it a source of indispensable material. Thanks are also due to Graham Millson for the front cover design and the drawing of Staniforth Road bakehouse. I must not forget the many typists who produced the material in readable form.

HOWARD HILL

Contents

Illustrations

To my wife Mary who is no mean baker

Bread to the hungry
Land to the peasants
Peace to the Nations
Bread to the hungry.

MAYAKOVSKY (1893–1930)
'Message of October'

Introduction

This is the story of the founding, growth and development of the seven Fletchers Bakeries, all but one of which were sited in Sheffield.

The first one was started by George Henry Fletcher at the end of the nineteenth century in a back-street slum house in Sheffield's east end. It was manned by its owner who did everything from fetching the flour and yeast to mixing and baking the bread, and then hawking it in two great baskets, one on each arm, round the adjacent houses and factories.

The seventh and present-day modern plant bakery, still in the ownership of the Fletcher family – a rarity these days – occupies a three-acre site on Claywheels Lane, employing five hundred men, women and young people. It supplies one-sixth of Sheffield's bakery bread production.

The eighty years which separate these two events are years of human endeavour so characteristic of all that is best in the British nation. If credit must go to the bakery's founder, George Henry Fletcher, whose humanitarian principles so well known to generations of Sheffield people were the spiritual foundation upon which the enterprises were started, then the major credit for clothing these ideals with bricks, mortar and modern machines, so apparent in the last venture, must go to his son George, whose vision and unremitting toil has made the most outstanding contribution to the Fletcher story.

There are those who see a glaring contradiction between the bakery's success and the persistent struggle which George Henry led, supported by his son over a period of forty years, for a system of society which would return the full fruits of their labour to the creators of wealth. This story will show that there was no inconsistency between their practical activities and their philosophy.

George Henry was a man of compassion. He was not afraid of being denounced as a rebel – a much greater term of abuse those days than it is today. As the *Sheffield Independent* reported on 2nd December 1920:

> 'If a man is denounced as immoral, as a rebel, because he fights injustice; as an enemy of society because he advocates collective ownership of those things which are essential for life and comfort; then I glory in the fact that I am a rebel.'

He suffered for his beliefs. Twice he was sent to jail because of them; the first time for insisting on the freedom of speech, the second time for making an alleged seditious speech. Within the limitations imposed by the system of private enterprise, all Fletchers' bakeries practised what their founder preached. The workpeople were treated as partners receiving more than trade union wages in an industry notorious for sweated labour. The bread and confectionery set a standard of quality unrivalled anywhere.

From the profits they accumulated capital, not in order to live a life of luxury and ease, but to modernise their bakeries while maintaining standards which have enabled the Fletcher enterprise to survive in today's fiercely competitive world. It is this which has preserved the independence which Fletchers' enjoys, and has gained it a reputation as Britain's most technically advanced plant bakery of today. A unique achievement!

I Early Days

George Henry Fletcher was born at Horncastle on 7th September 1879. He had three brothers and one sister. His father was a highly skilled shoemaker who moved to Retford in the early years of his family's life. Numbered amongst his customers were the aristocracy of the neighbourhood for whom he made the fashionable riding boots of the day. His shop supplied not only footwear for his neighbours, but had the reputation of being a centre of lively discussion.

Though most of the time he was a conscientious father, he had lapses during which he took to drink, causing much misery to his wife and family. Months would go by without a drop of liquor passing his lips. Then would start a bout of heavy drinking which lasted for weeks, taking all his money including whatever he could raise by pawning his tools. Suddenly the enormity of his weakness would strike home to him, and he would often seek help from his better-off customers to redeem his tools. Then he would work unceasingly to pay off his debts and meet his family responsibilities.

Little wonder that at an early age George Henry learned to fend for himself. At nine years of age he was awarded a certificate (dated 4th December 1888) for successfully passing the fourth standard school examination, and was promptly launched into the life of work which, in Victorian days – especially for the children of ordinary parents – was grim and forbidding.

His first full-time job was in farming, starting at six in the morning and continuing until dusk. His most painful farming experience was when helping to till the fields. The heavy roller, used to break up the lumps of ploughed earth, passed over him.

His next job was working at Ostlers, a miller and baker, for in

Six-sail Storcroft Windmill owned by Aaron Ostler, and destroyed by fire 7th September 1904. The nearby bakehouse was the first in which George Henry worked

those days it was the common practice to combine the operation of milling and baking. The mill was driven by wind power while the bread was made by hand and baked in a coke fired 'peel' oven. Both operations demanded a high degree of skill and plenty of muscle power. The flour, salt, water and yeast were put into a baker's trough. This was a wooden construction six feet in length, nineteen inches wide and one foot seven inches in depth, standing on short legs. Fifteen stones of flour which came in sacks weighing 280 lb (over two hundredweight) were poured along with the other ingredients into the trough; it was then mixed into one great irregular size and left to rise for an hour or so. It was extremely exhausting and skilled work. Said George Henry:

> '. . . men were bent over huge troughs, up to the armpits in dough, mixing it without leaving any knots. Often they caught

Nineteenth-century bakehouse

dermatitis, for which they received no compensation. After mixing they were so tired that they often fell asleep on the trough lid, which when the dough had risen, pitched them on to the floor. Then they knew it was time to lift it out.'

The dough was then thrown on to the bench, following which it was cut into pieces, weighed, moulded into a loaf, two at a time, one in each hand, and placed in the tins.

George Henry could lift a 280 lb sack of flour single handed. He was 'the finest moulder of a loaf I ever knew', said Mr Bert Slack, who worked forty-seven years, thirty as manager, at Fletchers' bakeries. He was President of the Student Bakers Association in Sheffield. The art of moulding a loaf was to make it without a hole in the middle. The tinned dough then had to be placed in the oven which was being heated up while the kneading was in progress. These ovens were built with a vaulted roof, the fire going directly into the oven through the flue, which was on the side of the oven. A small peephole in the oven door enabled the baker to judge the temperature of the oven – an operation requiring fine judgement and only acquired after considerable experience. Upon reaching the required heat and before the tins of dough were put into it the oven had to be 'scuffled out' so as to remove the dirt and soot deposited by the flames in the heating-up process. The scuffle was a long pole. Attached to one end by the means of a chain was an old sack. The sack was plunged into a bucket of hot water and swung around the inside of the hot oven. A tiring operation!

If the actual work was physically strenuous and mentally exacting, the hours of labour and level of wages were scandalous. Let George Henry's words speak for themselves:

> '. . . As an apprentice I lived in and there was another apprentice, one baker and the owner's son. We started work at six in the morning. After mixing the doughs and whilst the doughs were rising we had breakfast and went to clean out the stables and feed the horses; back to the bakehouse to work off the doughs; then after dinner we became roundsmen and distributed the bread produced in the morning. We usually finished about 5.30 or 6.00 pm, then the time was our own up to 9.00 pm; when we turned in at 9.00 pm we had to prepare the sponges for the next day. This consisted of removing from the oven two large pots of potatoes which had previously been prepared, these were placed in a tub and mashed, water was then added, and this was run through a sieve, and the sponges mixed. This usually took about 45 minutes, then we were free to go to bed.
>
> 'My wages were the same as the other apprentice, 2s 6d a week the first year, 3s 6d the second year . . . out of this I had to buy my own clothes and find pocket money.'

The baker's wages were twenty shillings a week. The average working week was eighty hours including overtime, for which they were never paid no matter how long they worked. In the larger bakeries continuous night-shift working was the custom.

Some idea of how poorly paid Sheffield bakers were can be gained when comparisons are made with the wages received by other grades of workers in those days. The wages of workers employed in Sheffield lighter steel trades – file, razor and scissor industries – averaged thirty to thirty-three shillings a week. The average earnings of a skilled engineer were thirty-five shillings a week. In some of these industries overtime payments had been won. If ever an industry warranted the description 'sweated' it was baking!

George Henry's next job was working as an improver at a bakery in Derbyshire. His wages were eighteen shillings a week starting at 5 am and finishing around 5.30 pm. Starting time on Fridays was 12 midnight working until all orders were completed on Saturday, usually around 12 noon to 1.00 pm. He no longer acted as a roundsman, but had the task of looking after three horses, Sundays included.

He found work in the baking industry so unendurable that he decided to try mining. For a time he worked at Grasmere Pit in Derbyshire. If anything, conditions were worse. So though bakers were known – to use George Henry's graphic phrase – as the 'white slaves of England', he reluctantly returned to the baking industry. Thus he settled for a working life in a calling the beginnings of which can be traced back to the Stone Age. So vital has bread proved to human existence that it has earned the description 'the staff of life'. Today it supplies an average of one-quarter of man's energy requirements and in the case of those engaged in hard physical labour, forty-five per cent. Little wonder that the baker and bread should have been at the centre of man's turbulent history, both his joys and his sufferings. It has entered into folklore, pagan and religious festivals, and mythology. It has caused riots and revolutions. Who is not acquainted with the supposedly inane remark of the executed French queen Marie Antoinette, who on arrival in France in 1770 and on being informed that the country folk had no bread replied, 'let them eat cake'?

Sheffield too has had its bread riots, and a poet who acquired fame for his verses which assisted the struggle to reduce the price of flour. On 18th May 1812 there was a demonstration in Sheffield against the soaring price of bread. 'Jacky Blacker', a tailor, carried a pole with a penny loaf dipped in blood on top, and a sign which read 'Bread or Blood'. Their demand was that the price of flour – which had soared to seven shillings a stone – should be reduced to three shillings. Ebenezer Elliott, who lived from 1781 to 1849 in and around Sheffield, became known as the Corn Law Rhymer. He wrote condemning the Corn Laws, which had existed for a number of centuries before they were repealed in 1846. They imposed a duty on imported corn, thus giving British-produced corn a price advantage in the home market which bolstered the profits of the landed gentry. In 1815 the laws maintained the price of wheat at eighty shillings a quarter. After the laws were abolished the price of corn fell drastically. Here are a couple of Elliott's verses:

> Ye coop us up, and tax our bread
> And wonder why we pine;
> But ye are fat, and round and red,
> And filled with tax bought wine.
>
> ('Caged Rats')

He also vigorously protested at the adulteration of bread, which in those years was widespread:

> They mix our bread with bran,
> They call potatoes bread;
> And, get who may, or he who can
> The starved, they say, are fed.
>
> ('The Taxed Cake')

As a result of the widespread agitation the Corn Laws were abolished. Elliott's statue stands to this day in Weston Park, Sheffield.

But not all human activities associated with bread brought suffering. The most pleasurable of all, without which humanity would not have survived, is closely allied with it. The Greek goddess of the cornfield, Demeter, who instructed the world's first ploughman in the arts of agriculture, sending him out to teach the world, was one day at a wedding feast. Having over-indulged in wine, she took a fancy to Iasion, with whom she made love in a thrice-ploughed field. Whereupon her jealous brother, Zeus, father of her child, struck the unfortunate lover dead with his thunderbolts.

In more recent times, there are the words of the Scottish poet Robert Burns, author of many fine verses, none more charming than the one he wrote to celebrate Lammas Tide (meaning 'the offering of loaves'). Here it is:

Corn rigs, an' barley rigs,
An' corn rigs are bonnie:
I'll ne'er forget that happy night,
Amang the rigs wi' Annie.

('Corn Riggs')

II Kirk Street – First Bakery; Retford – Second Bakery

It was while working at Ostler's mill and bakery that George Henry met Kate, who worked in the house as a maid. She was three years his senior, a Sheffield girl born in the slums of Brightside. He married her on 11th April 1898 at the early age of nineteen years, the ceremony being performed in the Ordsall Church near Retford. Kate was a good wife, the mother of his four children, and for the greater part of his baking career a vital unpaid member at his various bakeries. For a few years before their marriage George Henry had been working at a number of different bakeries in Sheffield. After their union they decided to take up residence in Sheffield in the hope of finding a better life. So did many others, attracted by the high wages to be earned in Sheffield's steel, engineering and lighter tool trades.

Sheffield in those days was a boom town, supplying much of the steel and engineering products for a country rapidly being transformed into the workshop of the world. By 1850 there were well over two hundred furnaces, some of which produced forty tons of steel, supplying ninety per cent of the nation's requirements. Unfortunately Sheffield's prosperity was exceedingly ephemeral! When demand was high, work was plentiful. The steel and engineering factories worked flat out. It was not long, however, before the pace slackened as demand was satisfied, then sackings were widespread; poverty and distress settled on the city like a plague. Such a period was 1896, following two brief years of boom. Between 1899 and 1901 outdoor relief payments to the very poor increased fifty per cent. Hundreds of families were without food. Some would join together under one roof to save on rent. During the cold weather furniture was burned to provide a little heat. So acute were the sufferings of the poor that the consciences of the rich were pricked: Lord Mayor's distress funds were launched; soup kitchens were set up – for these were the days when state unemployment benefit was unknown.

Happy as the Sheffield people were to escape the widespread starvation of slump, boom was not without its problems! If sustenance was much less of a problem, there was little change in the condition of houses. Those attracted to the town by the prospect of work and wages had to live somewhere, and though building of new dwellings went apace they never satisfied needs. This resulted in gross overcrowding. The situation was further aggravated by the location of these houses, the vast majority being built cheek by jowl with the factories. Though this reduced time and expense spent in travelling to and from work, it resulted, in times of boom, in the air being polluted by clouds of inky black smoke which blotted out the sun from the tightly packed back-to-back slum houses. This earned Sheffield the unenviable title of 'the city of the dreadful night'.

Such was the town into which the newly-wed Fletchers, high with the hopes of young love, moved at the turn of the century. They rented a house in Danville Street which is situated on the north-western fringe of Sheffield's east-end factory belt. Unfortunately, tragedy struck in the first week they moved to Danville

'City of the Dreadful Night': Atlas works, Sheffield

Street. Harry, only a few months old and their first-born, died. To add to their misfortunes George Henry was having his trouble at work. He was employed as a baker by the firm of Simmerson, whose bakehouse was situated in nearby Clun Road. The bakery employed four table hands who received twenty-two shillings a week and a foreman who received thirty shillings. Though regular overtime was worked it was never paid for. Work started at 12 midnight on Sunday finishing around 1 pm on Monday. This continued throughout the rest of the week except Friday when starting time was five hours earlier, finishing if they were lucky at 12 noon on Saturday. A working week of eighty hours was quite common in all bakeries in this period.

This produced a quite unexpected situation on the occasion of Queen Victoria's visit to Sheffield when she officially opened the town hall on 21st May 1897. A regal welcome was put on for the occasion. There were triumphal floral arches spanning many of the city streets, including High Street, Blonk Street and Pinstone Street; Venetian masts dressed to represent palms were everywhere. Streamers and bunting were hung from all the buildings, and Marples pub in Fitzalan Square was 'a veritable flower garden'. Even the works of Cammell's down Brightside Lane were highly decorated; the *Sheffield Telegraph* offices were all spruce after a new coat of paint. The overworked bakers were to be given a special treat. One master baker had hired a wagonette to convey his workpeople round the ostentatiously decorated streets. Unfortunately George Henry and his work mates saw none of this. After baking the bread and cakes to feed the fifty thousand school children assembled in Norfolk Park they fell asleep en route.

Simmerson, George Henry's employer, was an extremely religious man. Suffering no qualms of conscience he displayed in his bakehouse extracts from the Bible. One of the displayed texts aroused a riposte he never bargained for. 'The Wages of Sin are Death' it declared, to which one of his lowly paid workpeople added: 'The wages of a journeyman baker are a bloody sight worse'.

It is not surprising, therefore, that a man of George Henry's calibre should decide to do something about these unbearable conditions. Like many others in those days he was an active trade unionist, joining the Bakers' Union which, while it earned him the

Queen Victoria's visit, 1897: ostentatious decorations which George Henry and his workmates never saw

whole-hearted approval of his oppressed workmates, brought a torrent of abuse and opprobrium from the employers and all those who they were able to influence by means of the press and pulpit. Early in his career at Simmerson's he was promoted to the rank of chargehand which increased his wages from twenty-two shillings to twenty-five shillings. But George Henry was a man of principle! Never, throughout the seventy-nine years of his life, was he ever bought off by money; he did what he thought was right and just. What is more he was always out in front, fearless and courageous, often taking the knocks and suffering in consequence. So it was at Simmerson's. The Bakers' Union decided to try and obtain a sixty-hour working week in all Sheffield bakeries. The Master Bakers promptly rejected this, whereupon the union decided to take strike action. Mr Simmerson, anxious to avoid any disruption of his business, offered what he thought was a compromise. He proposed a reduction of the working week if in return his employees would accept a two-shillings cut in wages. So disgusted was George Henry that there and then he handed in his notice.

This was the end of an era for him. Never again did he work for an employer. It was not a matter of choice but of necessity. For many months he tried to get a job in and around Sheffield but Simmerson, for all his piety, made sure that none was obtainable.

Kirk Street – The First Bakery

Adversity often brings out the best in men and women. So it was with George Henry Fletcher. Now married, instead of sinking into the slough of despair and seeking the only aid available to the poverty-stricken in those grim times – the workhouse – he decided to strike out on his own. Little did he know the consequence of that decision – not only for the succeeding generations of the Fletcher family or for the baking industry, but especially for the workforce in Britain today.

Aided by his friendly working-class neighbours, not much better off than himself, he decided to start up in the bakery business. He acquired six bread tins which he distributed out to near neighbours who, after mixing their own dough and moulding it into a loaf, placed it into the tins which George Henry then collected and baked in his house oven. Gradually, with poverty never far from the door, he managed to purchase more bread tins, usually six a week until the oven capacity in his own home was insufficient to meet the bakery requirements of his customers. So the next-door neighbour, Mr Fields, ever-anxious to help, loaned him his oven. Eventually two house ovens and two gas ovens were in use.

It was at this juncture that the first opportunity to move forward presented itself. The 'goodwill' of a nearby cookshop, 129 Gower Street, became available for purchase. It was close enough to the steel works for some of the workers to come and purchase their dinners. George Henry was keen to have it, but unfortunately he did not have all the capital required. His next-door neighbour, Mr Fields, offered to help by lending whatever cash he had. Still it was insufficient; then one of those acts of generosity typical of many ordinary folk came to the rescue. Mr Fields fetched his barrow from his allotment and wheeled his wife's sewing machine to a nearby pawnshop which realised sufficient money to make up the deficiency. It was a grateful family which took over the business at

129 Gower Street.

Shortly after the business started to thrive, George Henry repaid the loans, but he still wanted to push ahead with the bread-making side of the enterprise. It was then, in the year 1900, that he started the first of the seven Fletcher bakeries. It was situated in Kirk Street only a stone's throw away from the house in which they lived. The man from whom George Henry rented it considered the place a dump: it had been empty for ten years; it had no living accommodation. 'If you can do anything with it, it's yours', he said. In it was housed a peel oven.

Nothing daunted, George Henry made a start. He had plenty of previous baking experience and now he wanted to make and sell his own produce as well as loaning out tins and baking for the local housewives. He cleaned out the place and assembled all the materials, which included two big baskets, one for each arm. From then on he became a familiar figure outside the nearby works gates at dinner time, and knocking on the doors of neighbouring houses selling the loaves, breadcakes and teacakes he had baked only a few hours earlier.

It was not long before the quality and freshness of his products gained him new customers, through the best advertising medium ever devised – word of mouth. It must be remembered that for centuries, unscrupulous bakers had resorted to many shady practices in order to make 'a fast buck'. Allum, a substance quite injurious to health, had been put in flour so as to make it white. It was not unknown to add dried china clay so as to increase the weight of flour. In fact so widespread were these malpractices, in all countries, that laws had been made to stop them. Centuries ago a baker in Egypt who sold bread adulterated or underweight was nailed by his ear to the post of his bakehouse. In Turkey during the eighteenth century when the price of bread went up they hung a baker or two. In England they were treated a little more leniently. Even so the first law controlling the price of bread was introduced in 1266.

Needless to say no such fate ever befell George Henry, nor for that matter to any of the succeeding Fletcher family. To deceive a customer with an inferior or underweight article was completely alien to George Henry's philosophy. And how well has this outlook rewarded him; it is one of the cornerstones of the Fletcher success story. As his competitors have so willingly acknowledged, the

Fletcher bakeries have always used the finest flour obtainable. George Henry was a man of many wise sayings, two of which are very appropriate to these early years of his business venture. 'The finest bread improver is best butter, if you can't afford it use lard'. From Kirk Street to Claywheels Lane lard has always gone into the Fletcher loaf. 'Milk is better than water', so milk is one of the constituents.

Little wonder that demand began to grow. Yet George Henry had a problem. In addition to running a growing bakery business, he was actively engaged in the early Socialist movement of those days, and was adopted as socialist candidate for the Burngreave Ward in the municipal elections of November 1905. Thus on most days he was engaged up to eighteen hours either baking and selling his bread, or in the political activities of a young socialist movement that was reviled and abused by the ruling circles of the day. He solved his problem in a typical Fletcher way – by technique! It was very primitive and crude, but it enabled him to move forward: he acquired a tricycle upon which was fastened a large box, replacing 'shanks pony' and the two large bread baskets. This enabled him to move farther afield into the working-class areas of Carbrook and Tinsley, some five or six miles away from his bakehouse. It was not long before the man-powered contraption was replaced by an independent source of power – a pony and dray.

Disease and Death

Life in Sheffield's east end was no bed of roses even for a family where the next meal was assured. Disease was rife in the closely packed smoke-ridden atmosphere of Sheffield's slum area. Particularly at risk were the children – in 1901 half of all deaths were of children under five. The younger they were the more vulnerable, with over one in four of all infants under one dying. Diphtheria, measles and whooping cough made no distinction between the families of the employed and unemployed. The worst killer of all was 'summer diarrhoea'. A hot summer brought death to hundreds of the very young, the death rate being three times greater than for any other disease. What is more, during the years 1894–1903 the death rate was twice as great in Sheffield as it was in England generally. To give the modern reader some idea of what this meant just let me compare infant mortality in those days with

1973: the chances of survival for a child under one year old are now twelve times greater.

Florence, the Fletchers' second child, was born in 107 Gower Street; within two years and five months she was buried. George, the third child, was born 20th July 1904. Could he survive? That was the worrying question that troubled his devoted father and mother. They were well aware that if only George could receive the fresh air of the winds which blew from the heather-clad moors of Derbyshire and arrived sweet and clean on the lucky people of Fulwood, a great difference would be made to his chances of survival. Better still to live there where the chance of life for a child under one year of age was twice as great as it was in Sheffield's east end. But as the prospect of this happening was remote indeed Kate did the next best thing: whenever she could snatch an hour or so from domestic chores she took the five-mile journey and carried George into Sheffield's west end.

It was of little avail! Whatever good the fresh air did him was more than cancelled out by the ravages of contagious disease which swept through the closely packed slum houses of Sheffield's east end. January 1905 – six months after George's birthday – was a particularly grim month for Sheffield's poor. More people died than were born. This was not because of a low birth rate; more people were born then than are born today. It was because of the appalling conditions. Little wonder that George Henry and Kate feared for their child's life. Urged by the doctor to get him away from this disease-ridden area they decided in 1906 to abandon their Kirk Street bakery which by the dint of hard work was beginning to thrive.

Retford – the Second Bakery

They removed lock, stock and barrel to the cleaner air of Retford. It was here they started their second bakery, renting a very small shop and bakehouse. Though it had its ups and downs the business was not without promise, and within a short time George Henry had two assistants. Both lived in as part of the family. One of them, Arthur Goodwin, aged ten, started out as an errand boy; he was to stay with the Fletcher bakeries for the rest of his working life.

George Henry's customers were much more spread out than ever they had been in Sheffield, living in several of the surrounding

Horse-drawn bakers' van similar to those used by George Henry at Retford

villages. This necessitated two horse-drawn vans to reach them. While the bulk of the customers were ordinary housewives, one or two were small shops and hotels; on Saturdays Kate ran a market stall. After a time although George's health took a distinct turn for the better the business was somewhat shaky. In an effort to cut costs one of his assistants was compelled to find another job.

All the customers were more than pleased with George Henry's fare, but as often happens some were not so keen to pay, especially if it could be got 'on the slate'. Numbered among the bad payers were some of his 'best' customers. Christmas, usually a boom time for bakers, was in 1907 a particularly trying one for the Fletchers. Fortune struck George Henry its most cruel blow. His van, in addition to the everyday products, was crammed full of those little goodies which marked out the season of cheer and goodwill. He was driving it alongside a canal when a coal cart a short distance away tipped off its load with a loud swoosh! George Henry's horse took fright and reared up in panic. The loaded van, animal and driver were pitched headlong into the canal. Fortunately he rescued the horse, but the van and its valuable contents were a write-off. That Christmas was anything but a merry one for the Fletcher household!

Try as they may, weighed down with unpaid debts – one of the worst being a big hotel – the victims of an unforeseeable misfortune, they had little choice but to return to the city which had brought both sorrow and fortune. It was with some trepidation that the decision to do so was taken. Young George's health was now much improved, but was it good enough to withstand the rigours of life in a working-class slum area of Sheffield? That was the burning question. They decided to chance it. Some twenty years later he paid off all his creditors at the ill-fated Retford business.

III Gower Street – Third Bakery; Staniforth Road – Fourth Bakery

Instead of returning to Sheffield's smoky disease-ridden east end the Fletchers rented a house in the north-west suburb. Here they hoped to get the best of both worlds: fresh clean air and the hoped-for benefits of employment. It was not to be!

George Henry was no armchair philosopher urging others to do what he was not prepared to do himself. Quickly he found himself leading a struggle for free speech. The Sheffield City Council had banned public meetings in parks. On more than one occasion George Henry and his socialist comrades had defied the ban. He did so at a meeting in one of the city parks held at the end of May 1908. For violating this city council bylaw he was charged and hauled before the city magistrate on 17th June. He received a prison sentence of fifty-six days to be served in Wakefield jail. A prison regime is very strict – especially when the food is rotten and medical facilities are primitive. George Henry bore it with fortitude. At least he acquired one skill of which most men are ignorant – they taught him how to knit!

His wife Kate had her problems too. The enforced absence of a breadwinner meant that somehow or other she had to find the means to live. She was also in the final stages of pregnancy. Leonard, their fourth child, was born while his father was incarcerated in His Majesty's State Prison. If George Henry was blacklisted for his trade union activities when he had earlier packed in his job at Simmerson's, just try and imagine what his prospects were after returning from jail in August 1908. Now he was a public figure revered by many ordinary folk, feared and hated by the employers. So once again the Fletchers were faced with the inevitable – either make another attempt to restart the business in the locality where the Fletcher reputation was high, or starve.

Gower Street – Third Bakery

The closing months of 1908 saw the Fletchers back in Gower Street launching out on their third bakery venture. This time it was a double-fronted shop window: numbers 107 and 109 Gower Street. The only useful aid was an oven, everything else vital to the task of bread-making was missing. In desperation Kate made a forlorn journey to Retford in an effort to collect some of the money owing to them. It was in vain.

They struggled through with the aid of all those good-hearted common people – themselves not far from poverty's door – who felt a deep affection for George Henry. Somehow they managed, but not before another of the Fletcher children died in 1909. This time it was Leonard. Thus the survival rate in this household was one in four. Grief quickly gave way to a determination that the sole survivor, George, was going to live. It was not long before the combined efforts of George Henry and Kate pulled them through. Many people, far beyond the ranks of those who admired George Henry's political activities, eagerly bought his top-class bread and confectionery, and also made full use of the service which many bakeries in those early days provided of baking the housewives' home-made dough. A charge of one half-penny a tin was made, a rate far cheaper than it cost them to bake it at home.

Staniforth Road – Fourth Bakery

With business improving both George Henry and Kate were anxious to make yet another effort to escape from the atmosphere of Gower Street. Their small successes were tinged with too much sadness brought on by the physical conditions of the area. Yet the hard knocks of life had taught them a valuable lesson. Move away, yes; but retain the physical contact with the common people. That was the hallmark of success for a business which more than most depended for its survival on the goodwill of ordinary folk. So 311, Staniforth Road became their fourth business venture. They moved there in 1912, living over the shop, which fronted on to the main thoroughfare. At the rear, across a small backyard, was situated the bakehouse. This housed the oven which had two chambers, one above the other, each capable of holding fifteen stones of flour made into dough – a total of 860 two-pound loaves.

While the bakehouse at Staniforth Road was being got ready for operation it was necessary to continue baking at Gower Street. George, now eight years of age, was a scholar at the nearby elementary school. After school hours, as he got older and grew stronger, he was increasingly pressed into performing the most irksome tasks of a virtually non-mechanised bakery. To him came all the rotten jobs: shovelling the coke, which came in two-ton loads and was tipped out in the street, into the bakehouse; fetching the yeast from the railway station; helping to grease the bread tins.

The fourth bakery – Staniforth Road

With the move to Staniforth Road, and before it was fully operational, his duties suddenly increased. To him and Arthur Goodwin, who after the business restarted in Gower Street had rejoined them from Retford, fell the much more onerous task of transporting, every day, the finished products from Gower Street to Staniforth Road – a distance of three miles. Once a day a local butcher loaned them his horse and cart, but it was not enough. They had to make more journeys using large-sized baskets mounted on an axle with a pair of bicycle wheels – an early and very primitive George Fletcher invention. A school chum recalls that George was considered to be a master builder of these schoolboy 'trollies', making them out of old packing cases. After completing his numerous bakehouse duties he along with other schoolmates could be seen madly careering down the inclined streets near the bakehouse.

On one occasion the grossly overloaded 'trolly', going over the bridge spanning the canal at Attercliffe, collapsed, though fortunately not with the same disastrous consequences which attended George Henry's accident at Reford at Christmas 1907. They salvaged the bread and the crippled 'trolly', which George repaired. It was again constantly pressed into service delivering bread to nearby customers.

He had one particular schoolboy friend, Walter Fields, son of the Mr Fields who befriended George Henry when they first moved to Sheffield at the beginning of the century. Walter was George's chief assistant. He recalls George also making a pair of roller skates; 'He was so mechanically minded', says Walter Fields.

The First World War

Teething troubles over, the business began to expand, and they waved a much relieved farewell to the sad experiences of Gower Street.

War clouds were gathering over Europe. On 12th August 1914 they burst with a ferocious explosion on the battlefields of Flanders. The Sheffield City Battalion was wiped out almost to a man. At home, shortages occasioned by the dual effect of the German U Boats' blockage of Britain's ports and the utter incompetence of the Government to ensure fair distribution, resulted in the essentials of life being extremely difficult to obtain. In those better-off areas where money was no problem supplies were plentiful – not so in the working-class districts where foodstuffs were in very short supply.

As many factory workers were cajoled into the army by the jingoistic recruiting campaign, the factories faced with growing demands for munitions were desperate for replacements. Men, women – many of them unskilled – flocked in as dilutees, provoking widespread resentment, which in November 1916 burst into strike action. The result was that skilled engineers had to be released from the army.

Nevertheless Sheffield working people, accustomed to 'bread and scratch it' caused by slump, were now working flat out, and for five years, starting with 1914, Sheffield's workpeople experienced one of those rare occasions of almost full employment. This meant that practically all households were in receipt of wages – though between 1914 and 1920 seventy-one thousand people received outdoor relief. The National Insurance Act had been introduced a few years earlier in 1911; the first ever in Britain, it only covered a few industries. Employers and workers paid 2½d each per week and the unemployed adult received seven shillings a week for a limited period.

Though work and wages were preferable to slump, with its poor law and unemployment benefit, living standards of the employed actually declined in this period. This was because increased earnings never kept pace with the rapidly increasing cost of living, which during the First World War shot up two hundred and fifty per cent.

Queues for bread formed outside every bakery, especially in Sheffield's east end. The greatest difficulty was experienced in obtaining flour, much of which was now imported from overseas. The Government imposed restrictions: no bread was to be sold until it was more than twelve hours old; potatoes must be used to augment the flour. The potatoes that George Henry got were mostly rotten, in any case recollections of flour adulterated by potatoes and other cheap substitutes were too fresh in his memory for him ever to contemplate such subterfuges. Using them was completely contrary to the fair deal he had always given his customers. To comply with these Government regulations was, he considered, inhuman; nor was he afraid of authority, especially when the rich were able to evade the rules. He refused to comply.

The First Mechanical Aid

With customers attracted by the high quality of his bread, business boomed. Early in the war Arthur Goodwin joined the army, and to replace him and cope with the increasing demand George Henry made two further innovations. The most important was the purchase in 1915 of his first piece of mechanical equipment – an Artofex dough mixer which could handle fifteen stones of flour in one mixing. Before this, the mixing and kneading had been done by hand; now that they had a mechanical aid George Henry regularly baked eleven hundred loaves of bread in twelve hours. Not only was the mixer the first in a Sheffield bakery but it heralded a development in technique which was to have a profound effect in subsequent years on the Fletcher baking enterprise. Two mixings were sufficient to load the two-chamber oven. Now one of the industry's most exhausting operations had been mechanised; working at Fletchers was somewhat easier.

His second innovation was to employ more staff – two male bakers and, to help Kate, two women shop assistants, one of whom was called Blanche Moss. The shop opened at 8 am and its doors were open until midnight. One of the bakers was Jack Hawkesworth, Secretary of the Sheffield branch of the Amalgamated Union of Bakers and Confectioners. This, too, was not without significance, for Fletchers have always been recognised as the foremost trade-union bakery in Britain. Though a master baker George Henry was numbered amongst the most active members of the union. He frequently represented the Sheffield branch at union conferences and district committee meetings. Twice he was elected National Vice President, sitting on the National Executive Committee.

The Fletcher – Holmes Partnership

It was during his union activities that George Henry met Sam Holmes, who in the early years of the First World War was manager of the Huddersfield Co-operative Bakery. They had much in common, broadly sharing the same philosophy of life, and it is not surprising that they decided to team up in business. Sam Holmes joined the staff as an equal business partner at Staniforth Road, which was known as: *Fletcher and Holmes, Bakers and Confectioners*.

Yet despite their common trade-union principles nobody was more surprised than Sam when, travelling into Sheffield one day, he found the Fletchers' bakery closed. Its staff including the Fletchers, father and son, were manning a picket line outside Davy's bakery. The Bakers Union in July 1919 had called a strike in order to win a minimum wage of £4 for a forty-four-hour week. The strike resulted in an arbitration award of a five shillings a week rise for a forty-eight-hour week to adult bakers. The local newspapers, ever anxious for an angled newsy story, dubbed George Henry 'master baker on strike against himself'. But was he? His 'over the odds' payment of trade-union wages and conditions was one of the factors which from the earliest days has forged a relationship between management and men that has helped to play its part in the Fletcher success story.

One year earlier, in 1918, George Fletcher had left school. Not for him the bakehouse: he was too intimately acquainted with the gruelling hard work which in a very short time reduced able-bodied healthy men into flat-footed deathly pale wrecks. No less important was his flair for things mechanical. The attraction which the space ship has for the youngsters of today was held by the aeroplane and motor car for the young contemporaries of George Fletcher's generation.

One day he joined a queue of boys all eagerly seeking a job in the garage of M. C. Burnbys and Son, coal merchants of Bridge Street. Some were prepared to take ten shillings a week, others offered to work for nothing just to get the training. Young George decided to ask for fifteen shillings. His future employer, somewhat taken aback, enquired, 'Why fifteen shillings?' 'Because I shall be worth it', he replied. And he got the job. Though his first duties were making tea, sweeping up and cleaning down those early lorries, he was nevertheless fascinated. Quickly he learned how to repair and adjust them, so much so that within a few years he was promoted to the position of chauffeur mechanic. In those days of unreliability it was essential for the driver to have acquired sufficient 'know-how' to cope with the all too frequent breakdowns of early automobiles. His schoolboy friend Walter Fields recalls that 'old Hobson', the boss of Burnbys thought the world of George. Walter, too, shared with George his interest in machines, so he got a job as an apprentice at a Sheffield engineering firm.

Meanwhile the Fletcher family left the working-class district of Darnall and bought a house close by the beautiful Mayfield Valley on the edge of Sheffield's west end: 67, Crimicar Lane. At last when not working they could inhale the fresh breezes which blew in from the Peak. They did have the problem of getting to and from work; young George solved this by becoming the proud possessor of a decrepit motor bike and sidecar. Together with Walter Fields he renovated it, making some modifications to the controls. They had plenty of hair-raising adventures on this early machine, one of which nearly ended in disaster when the throttle stuck during a trip.

A successful bakery business coupled with a house in Sheffield's upper-class residential belt has changed many a man's unpopular political principles. Not so George Henry. Never was he more heavily engaged in the working-class struggle of Sheffield's labour movement. It was the partnership with Sam Holmes which enabled him to do this. George Henry was to make and bake the bread while Sam made the confectionery.

By June 1921 George Henry was again in jail – serving a two-month sentence for making an alleged seditious speech in Rotherham on 29th May. The essence of his speech was a call for support for the striking miners, coupled with a plea to the police not to render help to the coal owners, but to pay back the debt they owed to those like George Henry Fletcher who a few years earlier had supported the police strike for increased wages.

His imprisonment was not without its lighter moments. One night the police turfed George Henry out of bed at 3 am to take him away to Lincoln Jail. The route lay through Retford, and going up Markham Hill the car broke down. All the driver's efforts to restart the engine were in vain. The policeman in charge demanded that George Henry give them a push. 'Not bloody likely', he replied; 'I don't mind giving a push if I am going away from the jail, but not when I am going to it.' So until another car was obtained he spent a few short unexpected hours with his father and mother who still lived in Retford.

On 26th July 1921 Sam Holmes wrote to the governor of Lincoln Jail enquiring when George Henry was due for release, as he had some important business problems to discuss with him. He was freed on the 30th. It seems quite clear what these problems were. George Henry's increasing political activities were more and more disrupting the joint bakery business. Shortly after, George Henry sold the business to Sam Holmes so that he was completely free to follow his political convictions. As will be seen in subsequent chapters this way of life was not to be permanent.

Cultural Interests

Before leaving these early years, reference must be made to a side of George Henry's life which fills in the picture of the complete man and which as had its influence on subsequent Fletcher generations. Committed as he was to activities which would alleviate the sufferings of the common people; ever conscious of the need to supply the necessities of life for his family which in the early years were never far removed from the poverty line – George Henry nevertheless was attracted by the finer things of life. He was an avid reader of books, appreciating good literature as well as the serious works which probed deeply into the whys and wherefores of social inequalities. He enjoyed good music and in the brief moments of relaxation, usually after Sunday tea, he and Kate would spend a few hours with friends listening to the music on the early gramophone – an instrument invented in 1894.

He wanted others to share these joys, which is why he gave unstinting support to the Sharrow Glee Singers, a choir which was largely made up of members of the Sheffield labour movement. They have gladdened the heart of many an audience at political meetings and brought some relief to the patients in the local hospitals.

It is not therefore surprising that his son George should early in life share his musical appreciation. While they were still living at Darnall George learnt to play the piano, an accomplishment which he kept up for the rest of his life. The business was never far away from the instrument, loaves of bread being stacked on top of the piano. Early in his teens he joined the Sharrow Glee Singers, which shaped his future in more ways than one.

IV Middlewood Road – Fifth Bakery; Penistone Road – Sixth Bakery

The guns were silent over the battlefields of Europe. The enemy was defeated. The just reward for all who had helped to win victory was now due. What a vision of plenty had been conjured up in the breast of the ordinary people by that master of oratory David Lloyd George who, in return for the sacrifices of the First World War, had promised a land fit for heroes to live in. But the people's expectations were soon dashed! Reality was totally different. Between the two wars, from the winter of 1920 until the rearmament boom of the late thirties – a period of fifteen years – unemployment, which decades earlier had blighted the lives of ordinary Sheffield people, now brought even greater misery and despair.

By March 1921 thirty thousand Sheffield workers were out of work, over one-third of them being men demobbed from the armed services. During the two stoppages of that year – the miners' strike and the engineers' lock-out – the number of unemployed reached sixty-seven thousand and sixty-nine thousand respectively. Employment prospects in Sheffield were worse than for any other large town with an insured population of one hundred thousand or more. As a consequence poverty was widespread and endemic. During the worst periods of slump some twenty per cent of all working-class households lived on, or below, the poverty line. As in the past it was the dwellers of Sheffield's east end who were the chief sufferers, with one-third of all working-class children under fourteen existing in dire poverty.

Little wonder that George, the sole surviving offspring of the Fletcher household, and now nearing manhood, should view with some apprehension his prospects of a happy and prosperous future. Having a first-hand experience of the arduous life of a baker he was no more keen now than he was when starting work, to follow in his father's footsteps. Nevertheless the alternative prospects seemed even more forbidding. Many hours he pondered the problem. What was the best course to follow? To remain an employee of a private employer risking all the hazards of unemployment, or to launch out on his own in the hopes of forging a better future?

However, the situation which confronted him was different from that of 1918 when as a raw fourteen-year-old school leaver, equipped with little more than his enthusiasm to become an engineer, he had rejected the bakery industry. Now, four and a half years later, as a result of his employment at Burnbys he had acquired some practical experience of the internal combustion engine. Naturally he raised the problem with his father. George Henry was more committed than ever before to a life dedicated to the well-being of his fellow men. In April 1922 he was elected a member of the Board of Guardians for the Darnall ward: the Board was an official body charged with the responsibility of administering the Poor Law. A year earlier he had helped to form the British Communist Party of which he remained a lifelong member, standing as its candidate in Sheffield local and parliamentary elections.

Many were the battles he fought, both inside the meetings of the Board and outside in the streets, to win better sustenance for the poor. On one occasion years earlier, in an effort to draw the attention of Sheffield's better-off to the plight of the poor, he had led an orderly march of six thousand unemployed to a Sunday service in Ranmoor church, which is situated in the west end of the city.

George Henry, reluctant as he was to be diverted from championing the cause of the people, was nevertheless conscious of his family responsibility. He reacted with his usual Yorkshire candour to George's dilemma: 'the only thing I can teach thee lad is baking, but if there is a repair garage for sale I'll try and buy it for thee.' The son replied, 'alright let's try and get a garage. If we can't we'll restart the business but I shall mechanise it.' Prophetic words indeed.

One day, father, son and Walter Fields went to see the Don repair garage in Hillsboro. Unable to contact the owner, they went and purchased a bakehouse and shop.

Middlewood Road – Fifth Bakery

On the 23rd April 1923 the fifth Fletcher bakery enterprise was

The Middlewood Road shop

launched. This time it was different from any of the preceding ones. The name George H. Fletcher & *Son* gives the clue to this difference. It occupied premises at 82, Middlewood Road, comprising a shop which fronted on to the main thoroughfare, with below a small room which was the bakehouse. In it was housed a small peel oven capable of baking four dozen loaves at a time, one small dough mixer, and an even smaller cake mixer.

On demobilisation Arthur Goodwin had returned to the Staniforth Road bakery. Now he joined them, along with Minnie Hawley who served in the shop. 'The boy Herbert' completed the staff of five which included father and son.

Even in those early days George was designated the somewhat grandiose description of being in charge of the 'Sales and Mechanic' side of the enterprise. His sales experience was nil; his only mechanical skill was the knowledge gained in his previous employment. Nothing daunted he set about his Herculean task with characteristic vigour. He borrowed a barrow from a nearby shop upon which he loaded eighteen loaves, and equipped with this primitive means of transport he canvassed among nearby shops for wholesale customers, delivering one loaf here and another there. Much later, in an interview with the Sheffield evening newspaper *The Star*, dated 18th May 1965, he recalled the 'thrill when I got three new customers on Penistone Road. That meant a little less pushing and a lot less puffing.'

If it was the drive of George Fletcher which won the new wholesale customers it was the quality of the products which retained them, for as every baker knows the housewife may buy the inferior loaf the first time, but to retain her regular custom demands the making of a product which none can better. As his competitors generously acknowledged, this, more than anything else, was the foundation upon which the rapidly expanding Fletcher Bakery enterprise was built.

Within eighteen months, by dint of hard work, George had built his first salesman round which was within physical pushing distance of the bakery. Now was the time to make his first real mechanical breakthrough. They purchased a Model T Ford car on which the baskets of bread were loaded. As the trade grew so the need for a van became all the more urgent. One weekend, helped by Walter Fields, he replaced the seats with a van body. Many were the alterations never dreamt of by Henry Ford which he made to this early vehicle, the most ingenious being a glass box mounted near the driving seat, fitted with spark plugs connected to the magneto and the cylinder plugs so that when the engine was running they sparked in unison. Should a cylinder plug fail the driver could see instantly which it was. Walter sent these innovations to the magazine *Motor* receiving five shillings and sometimes a pound in return, no small sum in those days. Little wonder was it that George Fletcher so highly treasured this first vehicle that thirty years later he transferred the registration number W 963 to his Rolls-Royce. That converted Model T Ford van was to George Fletcher what the inventions of the wheel and the axle were to early men.

Now he rapidly extended the wholesale side of the business. By Easter 1925 a second helper joined the wholesale side, Frank Brookfield, who in later years was to become Wholesale Manager. Within two months a further second-hand green-coloured van was purchased for twenty-five pounds, thus enabling two rounds to be established. Frank Brookfield recalls George Henry interviewing him for the job:

> 'These were the days when with the exception of postmen and police everybody was out of work. Prior to starting at Fletchers I had been out of work for two and a half years. I had been in Crimicar Lane Isolation Hospital being treated for tuberculosis. When he interviewed me for the job he told me that the first time he ever saw me trying to lift a sack of flour he'd give me my cards. Those were the days when lifting a bag of flour was everybody's job . . . I thought that was wonderful. I received one pound ten shillings wages when I first started. By week two it was increased by thirteen shillings and eight pence, and in 1930 I was receiving as much as a skilled baker and never lifted a bag of flour during the forty-five years I worked at Fletchers.'

Seldom in the history of job interviews can there have been one to equal this. It has characterised the Fletcher approach to all who have ever worked for them: the best wages and conditions paid anywhere in the baking industry, plus due consideration for problems of health.

Model T Ford, George Fletcher (on right) and van boy

George Fletcher's drive and mechanical bent were only part of his sales approach. He insisted on his sales staff looking clean and smart. His early salesmen were all decked out in peak caps, polished boots and 'leggings', an article of clothing unknown to modern generations. He also urged them to place their products in the shops' most eye-catching positions. Learning from the much earlier failure at Retford the salesmen were instructed to insist on payment at the time of delivery; there was no credit. This rule was observed even during the Depression years. It was not unknown for the van men to take the goods out of the shop if the shopkeeper said, 'I will pay you tomorrow'. Nevertheless the shopkeepers were treated with due consideration. One of the early van men recalls that there was no such thing as missing a customer, even if everything on the van had been sold. He must be visited and told, to be followed by an early call next day. Much later, during one particularly bitter winter, when all the roads were blocked with snow, bread was delivered to the village of Bradfield a few miles outside Sheffield on sledges.

It was not long before demand began to outstrip supplies. Within two years of starting, the staff had doubled. As the sales grew, both over the counter in the Middlewood Road shop and by the now mechanised wholesale trade, it became apparent to the 'Son' part of the enterprise that the small peel oven at the Middlewood Road bakehouse could no longer cope with the ever-increasing demands made on it. Nor, with the limited space available, was it possible to extend the production side of the business. This left the Fletchers with no alternative but to seek out a new site. The solving of this problem gives a clearer insight into the mental character of George. The immediate need was an oven, with ancillary equipment housed in a suitable sized building, able to meet the needs of the growing demand. George was thinking not of tomorrow, or even the day after that. He had ideas of a business, larger than anything then in existence, equipped with machinery which as yet was a visionary's dream. What is more to the point he had now gained sufficient confidence in his own mental ability to make such dreams become reality.

If proof is needed of this estimate one need go no farther than the next Fletcher venture located on Penistone Road.

Marriage and Relaxation

At this juncture it is necessary to break off from the business side of the narrative to fill out the picture of the human side of George Fletcher. For all his singleness of purpose he needed, and enjoyed, the finer things of life: the comforts of family life, the pleasures of good music. Nor did he lack the political understanding which made his father such a much loved and outstanding public figure in the political life of Sheffield. He joined the Communist Party in

1921, remaining a lifelong member.

In these early years he shared with many of his generation a deep love of the Derbyshire countryside. Whenever he could free himself from the demands of a young and expanding business he would be seen clad in shorts, shod in heavy Alpine nailed boots, striding out with companions over the rugged heather uplands of the Peak, or gently strolling along the well-known dales through which the rivers Dove and Manifold flow. On rare occasions, usually holiday weekends, he would set out on these jaunts after completing the busiest day in the bakers' calendar – the Saturday of a holiday weekend – surreptitiously bedding down for the night in an isolated farmer's barn, up early next morning eager to spend two carefree days enjoying the charms of nature in all her moods. It gave him new vigour to grapple with the problems of the business. These were the same friends who formed part of the Sharrow Glee Singers whom we have met in the earlier pages of this history.

Among these friends was the young, attractive Alice Coleman, a few months younger than George. A courtship started which saw its fulfilment in their marriage at the Sheffield Registry Office on 20th September 1926. Often in later years he quipped with that dry humour so well known to his acquaintances, that for him the two great tragedies of 1926 were his marriage and the General Strike.

They did have a honeymoon. And what better way was there of spending it than touring in a 1914 Darracq motor car with its canvas hood and its rear 'dickie' seat? It was the car which George had driven for his previous employer, which his father later purchased. Alice recalls how lovingly she polished it before setting out on that journey which for most newly-weds is the most memorable of their lives. The car was later to do service, in a most unexpected way, in the bakehouse at Penistone Road.

Penistone Road – the Sixth Bakery

Early in 1926 George H. Fletcher & Son purchased one thousand square yards of land from Tuby's, popular fairground operators. This was destined to become the site of a bakery which the *Sheffield Daily Independent* on 6th November 1937 described as, 'the magnificent machine governed bakery that brings visitors from all over the country and fellow craftsmen from America.' It was to be known as the 'home of the perfect loaf'.

The Penistone Road bakery

The 'then revolutionary' draw-plate ovens with the old-fashioned peel oven on the left

By April 1928 the first stage of the new bakery came into operation. Installed in the two-tier building, which covered less than one-third of the land, were two-deck Baker Perkins coke-fired draw-plate ovens which the *Sheffield Star*, 9th January 1965, described as 'then revolutionary'. This kind of oven permitted the whole baking surface to be withdrawn from the baking chamber thus facilitating both the loading and unloading of the oven – an operation previously done, one loaf at a time, by the use of the peel, a long pole with a flat piece of wood at one end. Thus more control over the baking process was now possible. Gone was the soot and grime of the primitive peel oven. Now the heat was conveyed by steam tubes.

The inside walls of the bakery were of white glazed brick which greatly facilitated cleaning, but the most important difference from the Middlewood Road Bakery was in the oven capacity. It baked three hundred large loaves every forty-five minutes – six times the output of the peel oven at Middlewood Road. To meet the dough needs of this greatly increased oven capacity required a mixer which made thirty stones of dough – far larger than anything ever used previously. It was sufficient to fill two draw-plate ovens.

Now the table hands in the bakery had the problems of satisfying the voracious demands of the increased oven capacity. Once again George Fletcher solved it by installing, over the next ten years, a number of machines and ovens which transformed the bakery from hand to machine operation. The first of these was a drum divider which cut the kneaded dough into uniform volume. Later an automatic first prover and a single spindle moulder – which shaped the loaves – was made into one unit by George Fletcher. From here the unbaked loaves went, via the final prover, to the oven. This operation called for considerable physical effort which prompted George Fletcher to construct multi-purpose setting racks holding three hundred units of tinned dough, where the dough completed its final fermentation before being wheeled up and slid on to the draw plates. It was then pushed into the oven.

When installing these early machines George Fletcher had first of all to win his father to recognise the value of them in the baking industry. Even though George Henry had installed a mixer in the Staniforth Road bakehouse, he tenaciously held to the view that no machine could mould a loaf. It was, claimed George Henry, exclusively a hand operation. The pieces of dough had to be rolled one way right up to the elbow, turned over and rolled the other. However, he did agree to go and view a moulding machine. Once he saw it in operation he changed his mind completely and purchased the moulder, which was installed in the new bakehouse.

In the early thirties he installed what has become recognised as the most revolutionary of all technical innovations, the wrapping and slicing of bread. The machine which carried out this operation is in all probability technically no better than many other of the mechanised processes, but its introduction into the Fletcher establishment – the first in Sheffield – coincided with economic conditions which made it an immediate and outstanding success. They were the years of the great Depression, with two-thirds of the working population on the dole. As we have seen poverty was widespread. In such times the hard-pressed housewife, to spin out the money, spent less on such things as expensive meat and fresh fruit, and more on bread which for a given amount of money contained more nutriment. In those hard times thousands of working-class families survived on bread and dripping. The 'penny dip' – a small bread cake sliced in half and dipped in gravy – was sold in thousands by small pork butchers. Fletchers supplied the bread cakes.

What is more to the point, the harassed Sheffield housewife, no mean baker herself, could scrape together the pennies needed to buy a loaf to feed her hungry family when she did not have the shillings to purchase flour and the coal to heat the oven. When sliced and wrapped the loaf retained its freshness much longer than previously, thus eliminating waste. More to the point was the price. It was the same as uncut and unwrapped bread.

These were the circumstances which made the Fletcher introduction of slicing and wrapping an instant success. The trade increased by leaps and bounds. By 1937 sliced and wrapped bread accounted for eighty per cent of all Fletchers' bread production. Little wonder the oft-quoted phrase, 'the finest thing since the introduction of sliced bread' has entered into everyday conversation. It had its origins in the hungry thirties. To keep pace with this phenomenal demand it was necessary to increase oven capacity. In 1935 the first travelling oven in Sheffield, a Baker-Perkins simplex, was installed, together with a cooler which took the baked loaves for a three-hour ride during which time their

Sheffield's first slicing and wrapping machine

temperature had dropped enough to be automatically sliced and wrapped. This cooling equipment was also built by George Fletcher. Finally the sliced and wrapped loaves were conveyed by travelling belt to the storage cupboards ready to be loaded into the vans for distribution to the shops.

The two small vans of the late twenties had by the late thirties become eleven large red vans each of one-ton capacity. They ranged for miles over the small urban areas and villages surrounding Sheffield. To house this sophisticated bread-making equipment, the handling and storage of flour and the loading of the vans, it was necessary to extend the buildings which now covered over fifty per cent of the land. This was the 'magnificent machine-governed bakery' to which reference has already been made. It was the brainchild of George Fletcher and won him the justifiable admiration of all who are familiar with the industry. He designed the layout, invented some of the labour-saving devices and at the same time improved many others. Walter Fields recalled one such innovation to me.

The moulded dough was conveyed by a belt which dropped it into the baking tin. Unfortunately, more often than not the dough missed the tin which necessitated posting someone at this critical point to ensure synchronisation. Many were the remedies tried to overcome this problem but none succeeded. Over a weekend when Walter Fields was staying at the Fletchers he was rudely awakened in the middle of the night by George shaking him and saying, 'Come on Walt, have got it.' Sleepily Walter replied, 'Tha's got what? Does tha know what time it is; get thisen to sleep.' 'No,' says George; 'we must do it straight away. Have solved it, we're going down tut bakehouse straight away.' When Walter was getting out of bed and dressing, George says, 'No don't bother wi' thi clothes. Slip thi coat over thi pyjamas and we'll go down straight away.' 'So a says what's tha' solved?' 'Ave solved the swinging tins.'

When they got to the bakehouse George picked up one of the new broom-heads which had long bristles on and fixed it so that when the tins came through they had to pass through the bristles which made them stationary, thus ensuring the dough dropped cleanly in. Walter Fields claims that Baker Perkins pinched that idea and

Eleven large red vans, Herries Road, 1936

patented it. There were many similar instances. Half a ton of rice flour a week was required to keep dry the belt upon which the sticky moulded dough was conveyed. George Fletcher hit upon the idea of blowing hot air on to the belt. Not only did Baker Perkins pinch this idea but they cheekily tried to charge Fletchers with having copied it from them. Furiously George was able to prove the boot was on the other foot.

Some have said he could have made a fortune had he patented his many innovations. But his motivation in life ran in other directions. Of course his first love was his business and he saw the only way to achieve success as being through mechanisation, for which the baking industry was in dire need. He worked literally day and night to make his ideas become reality, starting early morning and continuing until late. It was for this reason that the whole Fletcher family in 1927 moved from Crimicar Lane some five or six miles from the new bakery, to 60 Broughton Road, a five or six minutes' walk away.

His wife Alice recalls how he would wake up in the night and commit to paper the solution of a mechanical problem which he had been wrestling with during the day. Yet he never had a day's formal tuition in applied mechanics or machine drawing. While much of the mechanised equipment was bought from various machine suppliers, he was an ace at adapting what some considered to be useless and outworn machines. One typical example was the 1914 four-stroke Darracq car engine, which earlier had taken Alice and George Fletcher on their honeymoon. He adapted it to act as a standby to supply air to the oil burners in the draw-plate ovens, when the fan was unable to work due to power failure. He replaced the original radiator with a fifty-gallon steel drum.

Every machine was George Fletcher's concern. 'He was always mucky', recalls one of the early woman workers, 'and whenever you saw him in the bakehouse he had a grease gun in his hand.' He was a man of action not to be trifled with. Frank Brookfield has said of him that he could be your best pal, but when necessary he could still 'rollick' you. When he had done that you were back where you were before. He did not consider the 'cloth cap' a symbol of pure unsullied virtue; all have their endearing qualities and their not so endearing ones which have to be challenged, often giving rise to sharp differences. When George Fletcher had thought through his ideas and failed to win over the 'doubting Thomases' he would take more drastic action. One such occasion was the move from Middlewood Road to Penistone Road.

Arthur Goodwin was a highly skilled old-fashioned baker, one hundred per cent devoted to Fletchers, and sharing George Henry's high regard for quality. From an early date he was made bakery manager. Yet he did not share George Fletcher's enthusiasm for mechanisation, believing that the human hand and brain were superior in every aspect to the machine, a view which was to some extent shared by George Henry. It was for this reason that he resisted the move from Middlewood Road to Penistone Road. But George was not to be thwarted. One day soon after Penistone Road was already in operation he declared 'I'll get him down here', and he did. Over a weekend he moved the little peel oven to the newly opened bakery at Penistone Road. Arthur Goodwin had no option but to follow the baker's most important piece of equipment – the oven.

If it was the machine which produced the quantity, it was the men and women bakery workers, above all the Fletchers and Arthur Goodwin, who produced the quality. As we have already seen, George Henry rated the quality of his products higher than anything else. George, his son, for all his mechanical bent, never underestimated it either. The mechanical-minded are fascinated with the intricacy of the machine, but they do share with all other consumers enjoyment in the mouth-watering qualities and nutritional value of the finished product. It was no idle boast that Fletchers' products were unequalled.

There was no other firm in Sheffield which sold as many vanilla slices, lemon, jam and cheese tarts, as did Fletchers. 'People came from far and near for our lemon curd because it was home-made; I can see them now scraping the lemons', said Jack Habershaw, a retired van salesman. 'Customers would queue outside the shops for all sorts of cakes and great big boiled hams and Arthur's lovely barm loaves.'

Fletchers were the originators of the torpedo-shaped Wheaten loaf made from kibbled wheat, malt extract and Fowler's West Indian black treacle. When it was introduced in 1933, following months of experiments carried out by Arthur Goodwin, it took the trade by storm. 'It was absolutely beautiful', recalls an old-time baker, 'even suppliers of the ingredients couldn't make a loaf like it.' 'I sold hundreds and hundreds of Wheaten and hot brown loaves fresh from the oven in the south and west of the city. They did not want it down Attercliffe and Brightside, the old slum areas of Sheffield, preferring white bread,' said salesman, Jack Habeshaw, who in consequence was known as the 'brown bread man'. What a change from the days when white bread was the prerogative of the upper classes, brown bread being 'reserved [for] servants slaves and the inferior type of people to feed on.' (Lord Horder, *The History of Bread.*)

Tributes to Fletcher quality extend outside the ranks of his employees to, most importantly, his customers. In those days when competitions were the vogue, Fletchers swept the board taking many first prizes at exhibitions in London and Manchester. Flour millers, Sheffield's Food Inspector, bakery trade-union officials and even Fletchers' trade competitors have all added their praises. One well known Sheffield master baker said that Fletchers' quality was always on top. Another attributed the main reason for Fletchers' success to their high quality. The representative of Ranks, the flour millers, said Fletchers purchased their 'As you like it' brand of flour, which he claimed was the highest grade obtainable. The representative of another flour millers has said that Fletchers were the only plant bakers in the country which used 'top patents', a grade ten per cent dearer than the flour used by other bakers. Yet the price of Fletchers' loaves over the counter was the same as bread made by other bakers. A Yorkshire Bakers Union official has said the bread was the best in Yorkshire. No mean tribute, bearing in mind the Yorkshire housewife's reputation for home baking.

The cakes and confectionery are all made from the best ingredients obtainable: Australian sultanas graded five crown, Vostisis currants, both of which are the finest obtainable. Though the experts claim there is no difference between cane and beet sugar, old fashioned bakers maintained that custards made from cane are superior to the beet sugar ones, so Fletchers used cane sugars. The result: they sold many more.

Arthur Goodwin had his little idiosyncrasies. He jealously guarded the recipes of the Fletcher specialities. Edith Heard recalls how, when she started as a young girl in the 1930s, he would not permit them to write them down. As she said:

Girl confectioners, 1936

> 'Arthur would spell them out and you had to remember them. After being entrusted with these precious secrets we would rush out to the lavatory and write them down on scraps of paper concealing them by the elastic of our knickers.'

He had a similar attitude to the Wheaten. One day Frank Tuke, who started early in the 1930s, recalls George Henry saying to Arthur Goodwin, 'next week tha must take an holiday.' This Arthur was very reluctant to do, believing that he was indispensable. On the first day of Arthur's holiday George Henry appeared in a pair of white overalls brisk and early at 6.00 am saying:

> '"Now lad, thee tell me what to do and I'll do it." – I had only been there three weeks. At 10.00 am George Henry asked, "What time do we do the wheaten?" I said, "About now but I do not know the recipe." George Henry said, "Why not, tha makes it." I said, "Yes, when Arthur has weighed it I mix it." George Henry: "Does tha think tha can remember it?" I said, "I will try."'

Arthur was flabbergasted when he returned the following Monday and found that they had managed quite well.

Yet important as were the ingredients and the machines it was the men and women who mattered most. Without them Fletchers could never have succeeded. George Henry's personality aroused a feeling of devotion amongst all those with whom he had contact, including his workpeople. Stan Jackson, who worked at Fletchers for forty-five years, says of him:

> 'A real toff. A proper gentleman. I'll give you an example. I had not been at Fletchers very long. If anybody was on holiday George Henry used to come in and take his place. He did not come in as the boss, if it was the lad who was off, he did the lad's job. I recall one such occasion. There was a rack full of bread waiting and ready to go into the oven; he was the fellow to give me a lift with it, so I thought in this case the obvious thing to do is to go and ask Mr Fletcher if I should put it in. This is what I did. George Henry replied, "now lad you do what you think is right, it is up to you." Well, you can work with a man like that, can't you?'

This reveals George Henry's regard for his fellow men. As the owner of the bakery he was in a more dominant position than his workpeople, yet he did not take advantage of this. Of course, if based on his experience he believed he was right, he was never reluctant to intervene, but he did it in a way which strengthened a man's confidence, rather than weakened it. This attitude he had to all, whether his employees or not.

A Happy Firm

The wages and conditions at Fletchers were never below and were often more than the trade-union rates. Outside the bakeries owned by the co-operative societies, this was a rare exception. Bert Slack recalls how, when he reached twenty-one years of age in 1931, with much apprehension he asked for, and received, the adult trade-union rate which was three pounds a week. It was not unusual in those years of Depression to be given the sack upon attaining manhood. Bakers at Arthur Davy's, a well-known Sheffield bakery at that time, were receiving only thirty shillings a week, working continuous nights. In 1931 the average earnings in bread baking were

£2 11s 3d for an average working week of 48.3 hours* which is a rough guide to how trade-union rates of wages were ignored throughout the industry.

On the advice of her father, Mabel Thurlow, later to become Mrs Jackson, left her place of employment to work at Fletchers, because, she said, 'my father told me it was the best place to work at. I received twenty-two shillings per week at Fletchers and if I worked overtime I got paid. In my previous employment I got nine shillings a week for a twelve-hour day and no overtime payments.'

An entry in the wages book dated 16th August 1923 records Minnie Hawley who served in Middlewood Road shop receiving three pounds for two weeks' wages. The following week she was on holiday. Throughout the book similar entries can be read alongside every name. Most manual wage earners in Britain had to wait another twenty-five years before winning the right of holiday with pay. Nor did the introduction of machines result in any redundancies. When the moulder and divider machines were first installed in the 1930s slump, the bakers were worried stiff because they thought it was going to put them out of work. But it did not. In fact the original staff of five quadrupled by December 1931, trebling again by December 1937.

Fletchers was one of the first to have a canteen for its workpeople. This was started in the late 1930s. Both father and son believed that if the workpeople started with something in their bellies they would do a good day's work. So everyone in the firm could have a breakfast of egg and tomatoes, or sausage and tomatoes. Bill Coleman recalls how on Wednesdays he would go to a nearby fish shop and purchase fifty shilling's worth of fish. He would then call and collect from the greengrocers a fifty-six-pound bag of potatoes and sufficient peas. 'They would all make about fifty dinners for which a charge of sixpence was made.' They also got tea, bread and butter. A cup of tea was a penny, a refill a half-penny.

The Fletchers' concern with the welfare of their employees extended to the time when old age rendered them no longer fit to work. In 1937 the first contributory scheme was introduced. Each employee paid sixpence for every pound of wages received. Fletchers paid a similar amount. The representative of the insurance

* Department of Employment, *British Labour Statistics Historical Abstracts 1886–1968*, Table 39.

company, Liverpool and London Globe, who handled the scheme, has said there was no other scheme like it in Sheffield. In addition to receiving a weekly pension, a lump sum was paid on death to the next of kin. It covered everybody who worked at Fletchers, manual and non-manual. He recalls explaining the scheme to a meeting of all Fletchers' employees. Standing on a sack of flour, George Fletcher introduced himself thus: 'We are all fellow workers here, one of us has to be the boss. That's me.' The boss–worker relationship was not confined to work. They came together after work to share their relaxation. Often George Fletcher along with the more hardy vanmen went swimming in a dam on the outskirts of the city. Once a week there was a whistdrive to which husbands, wives and sweethearts came. The first prize was a very big chocolate cake.

It is not surprising, therefore, that the trust between the workmen and boss was as close as that which exists in any family. It is well illustrated by an incident related to me by Bert Slack. One week George Henry had come in to relieve on nights. Come Saturday, 6.00 am, after working from Friday afternoon, George Henry said, 'Well it seems we have finished lads.' Bert said, 'Yes, can I have my wages?' 'Oh,' replied George Henry, 'I haven't had time to make any wages up, lad. Here are the keys to the safe, go up and get three quid and I'll straighten up with thee next week.'

Being treated by the boss as a fellow human being and receiving the benefits of more than trade-union wages and conditions involved obligations best exemplified by Bert Slack's experience. After he had been working for only a fortnight at Fletchers, George Henry came up to him and said, 'It looks as if tha's going to stop with us, tha mun go and join the union.' Bert recalls it was not a question of 'will tha', but 'tha must'. So, next Saturday night he attended the branch of the Bakers' Union at the Hare and Hounds pub to be vetted, in order to ascertain if he was fit and proper to be a member of the union. It was the same with everybody else. None of them considered this constituted any restraint on their individual freedoms. It was an obligation arising from the fair treatment by their employer. According to a Bakers' Union full-time official, Fletchers were the backbone of the Sheffield branch of the Bakers' Union.

It was a happy firm, recalls one of the early woman workers. The atmosphere was enlivened with George Henry's whimsical humour, well illustrated by what happened to Mr Wild the milkman. He delivered milk to many households in the nearby streets, disposing of his unsold milk to Fletchers. Before putting the left-over milk in a tin he rinsed it out with hot water. One day George Henry was sucking his pipe down by the oven and saw some milk running out of a tin. He shouted to Mr Wild, 'Now then Wild, tha's put that milk in a tin which leaks.' To which Mr Wild replied, 'Well, Mr Fletcher, it was all right when I rinsed it out with water.' 'It must be bloody thin milk then,' countered George Henry. The management of other bakeries have continued to marvel at the intense loyalty of the Fletcher workforce. There is no mystery about it! 'You were not a number at Fletchers, you were a human being,' recalls Stan Jackson. That neatly sums it up.

George Henry's egalitarian principles extended to profits. He was not interested in amassing a large fortune as have been other prominent figures in flour milling trades. 'So long as he had his pipe and plenty of tobacco,' recalls a retired workman, 'he did not worry about much else. It was a great big pipe.'

In the first and second wage books which cover the period from the start of the Middlewood Road venture and extend to December 1931, George Henry never drew a wage. And later when he did there were others in his employ who received more than he did. George, his son, was in the early years in a similar position. Again drawing on the information gleaned from the early wage books, George's first wage was in September 1930. On that occasion Arthur Goodwin received one pound a week more than George. He not only paid the highest wages in the industry and unheard of fringe benefits, but it was George Henry's intention to make all who worked for him into shareholders. Two or three of the earliest workpeople did have shares and dividends were paid as the enterprise thrived. Yet the capital resources of the venture were always inadequate.

In the first year's operation at Middlewood Road they lost two hundred pounds. When demand grew, necessitating additional equipment, they were starved of capital. They did resort to the banks, but when the economic barometer showed anything but fine the financial institutions were very reluctant to lend a helping hand. George Henry summed it up in one of his many apt sayings –

'When it's fine they will lend you an umbrella, but when it starts raining they want it back.' Furthermore the Fletchers were always apprehensive of losing control to any institution, whether a bank or a big flour miller. This could have occurred had any of their shareholders decided to sell. As we will see later, there have been many attempts by the big concerns in the industry to acquire the Fletcher bakery.

At this time in order to keep the capital expenditure to the minimum they lived a very frugal life. They made do at the bakery with old second-hand machines which George Fletcher reconditioned. But as Rabbie Burns has said, 'The best laid schemes o' mice an' men gang aft agley', for it was arising out of these experiences that they decided, in order to meet the challenge of this fierce competitive world, to stop paying all dividends, ploughing the profits back into the bakery. This was a very wise policy, as subsequent events will show. This decision resulted in some of those shareholders outside the family objecting. Consequently their shares were bought back at a 'very satisfactory price'. In 1930 to protect the personal belongings of the family a limited company was formed. Just how competitive a world they operated in during the 1930s can be seen by an incident which scared all Sheffield's master bakers. A firm known as Daily Bread took over an old building, which had been used as a foundry in Sheffield's east end, converting it into a bakery. They produced a loaf which was sold at little more than half the price of a large loaf, much less than it cost to produce. Frank Brookfield recalls how he took out a van load of bread in the Darnall area returning a few hours later with scarcely any sold: 'I was nearly in tears.' George Henry was not easily frightened. 'There is one thing we are not altering and that's the price. We may as well play for nowt as work for nowt,' he said: an outlook common to all the Fletcher family. It was not long before the price-cutting war ended. 'Daily Bread' were using inferior flour and within a short time the cowboy firm folded up.

It would be unfair to place all Fletchers' competitors in this category, although as will be seen later one Sheffield competitor did try to cripple Fletchers. Nevertheless, with a few notable exceptions their production costs were lower than Fletchers because the wages and benefits paid were less than at Fletchers. They also paid dividends to their shareholders. Furthermore, many did not use top-quality ingredients.

George Henry never engaged in sharp practices with either his competitors or commodity suppliers, even though many of them held political views diametrically opposed to his own. He treated them with the same consideration as he did the more lowly. Two examples which are complementary illustrate this.

It was the usual practice during the 1930s to purchase flour sometimes months ahead of actual use – a practice known as 'forward buying'. In this way bakers were able to take advantage of the lower prevailing price levels. On one notable occasion this operated to the disadvantage of the bakers, the price of flour falling below the contracted price. Most of the master bakers of the day tried, and many succeeded, in evading their contractual obligations by threatening the millers with cancellation of all their future flour business unless they received supplies at the prevailing lower rates. Not so George Henry! He paid the higher price for the flour which the millers agreed to spread over a longer period than usual. This brought to light a practice which reveals him as a man of the highest integrity no matter with whom he was dealing. He would never sign a contract. He considered his 'word was his bond', which once given was always honoured. In fact if the supplier insisted on a written contract it was usual for the representative of the supplying firm to sign it on Fletcher's behalf himself. What other enterprise with no written contract would have still paid the higher verbally contracted prevailing price?

George Henry expected to be treated in a similar fashion. And woe betide any who violated his code of conduct. One Sheffield flour miller did precisely this by breaking such an undertaking, with the result that George Henry refused ever again to have any dealings with him.

George Henry had little time for 'paperwork'. He was always too busy baking bread, an attitude which finds a sympathetic response today. His office was a table in the changing- and rest-room, where he was assisted by a part-time clerk, Emmy Spencer. He had an old typewriter which the first full-time office worker, Miss Taylor – who started in 1937 – was unable to operate because it was so antiquated. He also had two books – the wages book and an income and expenditure book. This comprised all his office requirements. There was no cheque book. He told Miss

Taylor: 'We pay everything with cash.' Later on at Miss Taylor's suggestion an office was provided and a new typewriter and cheque book obtained, with all the other essential material.

Miss Taylor refers to George Henry as 'Grandfather'. She recalls him telling her how in the early days they came to engage accountants to audit the books. During the First World War they received an income tax demand which made George Henry say, 'that seems a lot, we'd better have experts.' So he walked along Bank Street in the centre of Sheffield, where most of the city's solicitors and accountants were situated, knocking on the first chartered accountant's door. After examining the books the accountant was able to see that neither George Henry nor his wife Kate who helped him in the business had taken any wages. Resulting from this audit he was able to reclaim quite an amount of money from the tax authorities. Later on George Henry and Kate together did receive around four pounds ten shillings per week.

Up to Miss Taylor starting, the whole of the weekly insurance stamp – including the workers' share – was paid by George Henry. Miss Taylor took this up with him. 'It helps the men' he explained; 'if I don't do it the business will start to pile up money.' But as the capital needs of the business increased he stopped this practice.

The discerning reader will have noted the increasingly important role that George, the son, was playing in the business, starting with the move to Penistone Road. It was not a question of a younger and more thrusting personality with newer ideas pushing an older man aside, though it must be said that George Henry was never as mechanically minded as was George, retaining many of the views based on the earlier handcraft practices. During the 1920s and 30s George Henry was more heavily committed than ever before in pursuing the struggle for his ideals. This as we have seen was dearer to his heart than becoming a successful businessman.The newspapers of the day were full of his outside activities which they reported in the news columns and in cartoons, and he was so respected by his Labour colleagues on the old Sheffield Board of Guardians, that they elected him as their chairman. At the Board Meetings he made many a fiery speech defending the poor. Outside, along with others, he was helping to organise street demonstrations with huge public meetings, fiercely resisting all attempts made by the Government of

George Henry Fletcher addressing ten thousand unemployed, Barker's Pool, Sheffield, 7th October 1931

the day to cut the relief payments and disqualify the unemployed from receiving the benefits to which they were entitled. He marched to London with the Sheffield contingent of the Jarrow hunger marchers. The *Sheffield Daily Independent*, 17th April 1927, described him as 'the stormy petrel of the Board . . .'. The less fortunate poor, those who were forced into the workhouse, became known as 'Fletcher's Pets', because he had won for them three blankets to keep out the cold, and for the old inmates best butter instead of margarine. Not a bad epitaph of which any man might be proud.

The General Strike of 1926 found George Henry in the thick of the struggle. He could well have gone to jail again for violating the Emergency Powers Act. He was saved by the efforts of Arthur Neal, a prominent solicitor and leader of the Liberals – for many years his main political opponent – who defended him in the Courts for nothing. The fine, which George Henry refused to pay, was collected from among his many supporters.

Thus it was that the onerous task of running the bakery fell on the not unwilling shoulders of the son. The advice of the older and more experienced man was always at hand and often sought. It is not surprising, therefore, that in 1938 George Henry, confident that the business was in capable hands, should have no doubts about taking an extended holiday. In the spring of 1938 he decided to fulfil a lifelong desire to visit his brother, a farmer in Ontario, Canada, coupling it with a visit to some of the biggest bakeries in the United States of America, whose head, the Vice-President of Short Mill Bakery, had earlier visited Fletchers' Bakery. However, at first the American Consul in London refused to issue George Henry with a visa, considering he was a dangerous Red who might undermine the American way of life. He only relented following the intervention of Sheffield's Labour Lord Mayor and the Labour Co-operative Sheffield MP for Hillsborough, the Rt. Hon. A. V. Alexandre. So it was that along with his wife Kate he spent a few months away from the bakery. When he returned he decided to retire, in later years telling the *Sheffield Star* (11th April 1958), that 'they seem to have managed as well without me, as with me, so I retired.' He was sixty-one years of age.

From his visits round the bakeries he brought back a machine which automatically greased the tins, previously done by hand. This had been one of the most detested jobs which was usually reserved for the young lads.

Four years earlier an only child, George Paul, had been born to George and Alice Fletcher. The social conditions in which he first saw the light of day were very different from those of his father and grandfather, as was the industry in which he was destined to play his part. Nevertheless, as the subsequent pages of this history will reveal, the fight which he had to make for survival of the Fletcher bakeries was no less acute than anything faced by his forebears.

V Penistone Road – The Second World War and After

The first word in a war is spoken by the guns, but the last word has always been spoken by bread.

HERBERT C. HOOVER, 31st President of U.S.A.

Among the many promises made to win the support of the British people for the 1914 war was that it was the 'war to end wars'. Within twenty years it was cast aside like an old shoe as the people were pitchforked into yet another major war – the second in the lifetime of many. What is more pertinent, it was against the same enemy, Germany, whose defeat had cost the British people so dearly in the First World War.

There were at least two major differences from the earlier conflagration. One was the absence of jingoism which was such a feature of the First World War. It was quite unnecessary, for following Hitler's seizure of power and the subsequent cruel repressions, few British people had any illusions of what their fate would be were he to conquer Britain. Secondly, after the gruesome experiences of the civil war in Spain, in particular the total obliteration by Hitler's dive bombers of the town of Guernica, it was now painfully obvious that the front line was no longer a 'no man's land' – the few hundred yards of territory separating the fighting armies. Now the civilian population was the target.

As Chamberlain – the British Prime Minister – made the declaration of war on 3rd September 1939, a fearful tension descended upon the British people as they awaited with trepidation the arrival of the Luftwaffe. The early months rolled by and nothing happened. Fear gave way to a mood of almost carefree laughter. It has been christened by some as the 'twilight war', by others the 'phoney war'. It was soon to be shattered, at the end of July 1940.

Hitler launched his merciless air raids on the capital city prior to mounting an invasion which no one had attempted for well nigh a thousand years. During the month of August and into early September the raids were continued with ever-mounting ferocity. Gone was the euphoria of the 'phoney war'. The British people waited with baited breath as the battle raged in the skies over London and South-East England. It was won due to the heroism of the air crews and the quality of the British fighter plane, the Spitfire.

The reader may be wondering what this has to do with the baking of bread and even more pertinently with the history of Fletchers: more than has so far been credited. It was Napoleon who said that an army marches on its stomach. Never was this more apposite than in the First and Second World Wars. And as we have seen, there is no article of consumption which, weight for weight, contains greater sustenance than bread.

In September Hitler, defeated in his first attempt at invasion, turned his attention to destroying the sinews of war – the munition factories and those who manned them. High on the agenda of Hitler's strategic plans was Sheffield, and well it might be, for as Professor Haldane wrote in his book *A.R.P.*, 'there is half a square mile of Sheffield which is more vital for the production of munitions than any other part of Britain.' In fact for the first eighteen months of war, the only drop hammer in the country able to forge the crankshaft for the Spitfire was located in Vickers' works down Brightside Lane. Hitler knew it. His radio publicist, the traitor 'Lord Haw Haw', regularly beamed it over the radio waves.

On the 12th December 1940 there was a beautiful crisp moonlight night as the heavy German bombers set course for Sheffield; the sort of night that lovers and bomb aimers relish. The pubs had only been open one hour when the high explosives rained down on this city so vital to Britain's war effort. By the next morning much of the city's centre was a shambles. So were some of the suburbs. But the vital drop stamp was intact. The bomb aimers had missed their target. They made another attempt on 15th December. Again they failed, but the havoc they inflicted was grievous. Killed were 668 people; ninety-two were missing; 513 seriously injured. Thousands of houses were damaged, many being rendered unfit to live in.

High Street, Sheffield after the air raids

No less serious for the struggle was the disruption of the services – especially water and gas which were extensively used in both the heavy and light industries of the city. Eight gas-holders, in the Grimesthorpe, Effingham Street and Neepsend Works, were completely demolished. Practically the whole of the city was without this vital fuel.

How fortunate it was that George Fletcher had used oil instead of gas to heat his travelling oven. Every other large bakery used gas and was out of production. Fate had also played another part. Hillsborough was one of the few localities where the water supply was virtually intact. Aided by the workers from the other bakeries rendered workless, Fletcher toiled as never before – twenty-four hours a day seven days a week – turning out the life-giving bread. Against the advice of the makers George Fletcher had speeded up the three and a half sack travelling oven, thereby increasing output. The shortfall was ferried in from the surrounding areas. The only time work stopped was on Saturday nights. Then George Fletcher, aided by whoever could be pressed into service, carried out the essential maintenance. His experiences in the early years of the bakery proved invaluable in keeping the plant running when machine replacements were virtually unobtainable.

Yet fickle fate struck again. This time not to help but to hinder. Five days after the second Sheffield blitz Fletchers was on fire. It was not by design but human frailty. The tanker driver delivering the oil had connected his delivery pipe to the full storage tank instead of the empty one. Quickly the inflammable liquid seeped through on to the oven which set it alight. Soon the bakery was a raging inferno as the oil pipes melted, releasing thousands of gallons of oil into the heart of the fire. The staff and firemen struggled manfully to put out the blaze. They did manage to confine it to one small area, a large hole in the ground which, before the installation of the oil-fired travelling oven, was used to store coke, and subsequently as the maintenance shop.

The morning after the fire was one of desolation! It completely upset the manager Arthur Goodwin who never recovered from the shock. George Fletcher, forever the optimist, considered it a good job. 'It was about time we had a clearout,' he said. It presented him with a marvellous opportunity to rebuild the ovens which would increase the bakery's production capacity and make possible the reorganisation of the confectionery. George Henry, not as optimistic as his son, came over from Leverton and said: 'but for the lads who work here I'd pack the whole bloody thing up completely.' He went over to the eight girls who came out to work the next morning and asked them to clear up the mess. In spite of the fire's intensity – it had destroyed the four ovens including 'Arthur's peel oven', which at the time was baking lemon tarts – the most important parts of the plant were still intact. These were the travelling oven and the mixing room. The confectionery was completely gutted.

Immediately following the catastrophe of the fire, George Fletcher set about the difficult war-time task of rebuilding the destroyed ovens. Within eighteen months the four burnt-out ovens were replaced by six draw-plate ovens, which were coke-fired so as to reduce to the minimum the possibility of further destruction in the event of enemy air raids. He again expanded the capacity of the travelling oven by redesigning the tins so that the number of loaves travelling through the oven was increased by 112, with the result that an oven which had a maximum designed capacity of eight hundred loaves each hour, was now producing a thousand: a total for a seven-day week of 150,000 two-pound loaves.

With the replacement ovens coming into production George Fletcher saw an opportunity to give his hard-pressed customers and his own staff a little something extra. During the whole eighteen months, while rebuilding was in progress, Fletchers had been taking their full allocation of raw materials. Huge quantities of sugar, fruit and dried eggs had been put into store. 'We are ready to start baking,' George Fletcher told the newly appointed assistant manager Bert Slack; 'make us as many fruit cakes as possible, that's the way to give the population something different.' Thousands of fruit cakes were sold, a rare war-time luxury.

It was not only the blitz and the fire that created problems for war-time Fletchers. As in so many other concerns all the young men and women under thirty were called up, except for a few essential exemptions. Those called up were replaced by men and women too old for military service, and with the traditional tolerance shown by Fletchers for unpopular minority views, some conscientious objectors were employed.

For the first time – at least in this century – women worked nights. A weekly payment was made by Fletchers to the dependents of all those called up – an act of generosity rare, if not unknown, in any other baking establishment. Though bread was not rationed until after the war, supplies of raw materials, with the exception of flour, yeast and salt, were limited by a system of allocation. Each bakery had to state the amount of materials used in the pre-war days. Fletchers filled in the necessary forms with a scrupulous honesty not observed by many of their competitors, who in consequence received a bigger allocation. Some ingredients such as cherries which helped to relieve the jaded war-time palate were no longer available, so substitutes called 'chellies' were used.

Conditions of war-time work in the bakehouse were well nigh unbearable, especially on nights when the city was most vulnerable. It was essential that not a chink of light was visible from the outside, and in consequence all the windows were tightly sealed. The ovens, being coke fired, emitted carbon monoxide which circulated round the bakery, causing everyone's eyes to run. Despite these trials all the workers responded magnificently. They worked during air raids producing bread – for which they were compensated with double pay, starting from as soon as the air-raid sirens sounded, whether or not they heralded an actual attack.

The hours of work were twelve and sometimes sixteen a day, to be followed by a night's firewatching. George Fletcher, to give the firewatchers some protection, converted a disused steel boiler into a protective air-raid shelter which was hauled on to the roof. One night, to relieve the tension, but especially the monotony of grated carrot sandwiches, the women surreptitiously made a huge meat and potato pie. Edith Heard, who seems to have been the prime mover in the project, collected together all the ingredients. A few of the women workers who had big families received quite a large meat ration, and they brought the meat. Others brought the potatoes, onions, carrots and relish. Edith, who was the mixer, accumulated enough fat and flour to make the crust which was decorated with about thirty pastry leaves. It was a huge pie, filling a container eighteen inches across and two feet deep. There were over fifty pounds of potatoes in it. The pie was big enough to feed between twenty-four and thirty people. Edith, recalling the occasion, said:

'In addition to mixing I operated the draw-plate oven, I therefore was able to put the pie on the draw plate and push it into the oven. When it was done I started to pull it out and the pie rocked on the oven bottom. We shouted Bill Coy the foreman to tell the lads that supper was ready. That was the first he had heard about the pie. His eyes popped out when he saw it. He demanded to know who gave us permission to make it. He played hell! – though that did not stop him having a helping. He said, "tha'd better see the gaffer or else we shall all get sack," but the boss really took it in good part. He ended up by saying "you never saved me a bit," but I had to promise not to do it again.'

The war was moving into its final stages. Like others George Fletcher was thinking about the future. He realised that once peace was established the opportunities for expansion on a hitherto unprecedented scale would arise, and he had every intention of trying to satisfy this. He realised this would never be possible at Penistone Road where due to overwork during the war the machines were worn out. The only course open was to replace them with new equipment, which was not possible at Penistone Road. During the thirties, when machines had started to replace some of the hand production, they had only been housed by building upwards and taking over the land which previously had been used for parking the vans.

There was land available, but a Bradford firm called Newbould, realising the potential in Sheffield, had in the middle 1930s installed a bread and cake distribution depot on Fletchers' doorstep. Daily they ferried supplies in from Bradford by articulated lorries. Quickly Newboulds realised that Fletchers were their main competitors, so they purchased all the remaining available land immediately adjacent to the bakery and would not sell any of it, even though they did not require it themselves. This made George Fletcher and his father suspect it was done to prevent any further Fletcher expansion. But as we will see later it turned out to be a blessing in disguise. At that time to accommodate the vans, Fletchers had been forced to purchase land which was separated from the bakeries by Newbould's land. They also rented for a short time a local publican's building which was used as the van maintenance department. To replace this a piece of land was bought and a small aircraft hangar erected on it.

It was not only George Fletcher who saw the opportunities in the post-war world. There were others in the industry who also realised that the British people were not going to be fobbed off for a second time with empty war-time pledges of a better world. This time the people were determined to take action to ensure that out of the ashes of the Second World War would arise a Britain very different from that of the 1920s. Aware of this mood all Britain's manufacturers planned for big and rapid increases in output – none more so than the baking industry! In the pre-war days, technology, then in its infancy, had been applied to this hitherto backward industry, especially, as we have seen, in plants like Fletchers; the result was that by 1938 twenty-five per cent of bread was made in plant bakeries.

Now preparations were made to bring more technology into the bakehouse, which resulted in great increases in productivity. The Bakers' Union claims that the output of loaves has risen from forty-five per man-hour in those days, to 666 in 1965.* Not everybody in the trade accepts these figures. Alongside this development another trend made its appearance with the formation of combines. It was started by Garfield Weston, a Canadian who came to Britain in 1934, founding the Weston biscuit companies and erecting new plants in many parts of the country. In 1935 he formed Allied Bakeries Ltd. This was the start of transforming baking into big business. After the war Weston acquired bakeries in all parts of the country and by 1954 his company had seventy bakery plants, to which he added another sixteen bakeries and nine hundred bakery shops in the next four years. These in the main were substantial concerns with considerable local trade. They provided more productive capacity, and even more important, greater outlets for the sales of his bread and cakes. 'His most spectacular acquisition was London's chain of ABC Tea Shops'. (Ronald Shepherd and Edward Newton, *Story of Bread*, 1957.) There were many others besides. He would acquire a string of such shops and bakeries, closing some of them down, selling off the property and transferring both the baking and the custom to other nearby shops and bakeries. By October 1976 he owned 1,778 specialised bakery shops and became the sole supplier of standard bread to the Fine

* Bakers Union, *Our History 1849–1977*, page 84.

Fare Group of Supermarkets which he owns. He also operates in nine hundred others.

It was not long before this growing empire of bakeries and shops came into conflict with the millers. Weston considered they charged him more for his flour than was justified, and so he started to import his own flour from Canada, which aroused growing resentment from the existing milling interests. In 1961 he acquired his own mills. The millers retaliated in like fashion, at the same time extending their holdings far outside both baking and milling.

In 1952 Arthur Rank (later Lord Rank) succeeded his brother James as Chairman of Ranks Ltd. The company began pushing ahead into banking and agriculture merchandise by buying many family businesses.

> 'In 1962 Ranks Limited acquired Hovis-MacDougal Company and changed its name to Ranks Hovis MacDougal Ltd. Six years later, the acquisition of Cerebos, another food group with its roots in Victorian times, brought with it a number of well known food brands. Simultaneously the company's agricultural interests were being extended with the acquisition of agricultural merchandising companies. Ranks Hovis MacDougal had become far more than a flour milling company under the chairmanship of Arthur Rank.'
>
> (*R.H.M. 1875–1975*, published by Ranks Hovis MacDougal.)

Spillers pursued a similar policy. Between 1954 and 1969 they had acquired seventy plant bakeries, forming United Bakeries, the baking division of Spillers, and in 1972 they merged their milling and baking industries with Joe Lyons Ltd and the Co-operative Wholesale Society. In both flour milling and baking the era of combines had arrived. 'The Big Three' (Associated British Foods, Ranks Hovis MacDougal, and Spillers French), supplied sixty-two per cent of all bread production. The independent plant bakers supplied eleven per cent, and master bakers twenty-seven per cent.

There are some 5,500 master bakers usually operating behind a shop, and forty-five independent plant bakers. Not all of the master bakers or the independent bakers are really independent. Some are tied to millers for flour supplies as a condition of receiving loan facilities. What is more, a sort of 'closed shop' operates for fifty-one per cent of the market in flour, because – as the Monopolies and Mergers Commission Report, *Flour and Bread*, July 1977, notes – 'each of the major groups required its flour-using subsidiaries to buy their requirements of flour from its own mills insofar as it was possible to do so.' What a contrast with the earlier decades of the century when a free market in flour existed and the master bakers accounted for fifty-five per cent of all bread baked!

Alongside this has developed a similar trend in retailing. It was Adam Smith, the eighteenth-century economist, who described the British as a nation of shopkeepers. And so they have remained until recent years. The corner shop – once the hallmark of Britain – is as outdated as the Hansom Cab in the era of Concorde. In the ten years ending 1971 the number of grocer's shops declined nearly thirty per cent. So great is the change that a new word has been coined to describe it. It is 'supermarket', a noun that does not appear in pre-war dictionaries. Now there is not a town in Britain without its supermarket; six supermarket chains account for one-third of all money spent on food. (*The Times*, 19 April 1978.) Some of them are owned by the big flour and baking combines.

This development has to be seen against the background of what has happened to eating habits in post-war Britain. The austerity of the hungry 20s and 30s has given way to the affluence of the 1950s and 1960s, and it is no longer 'bread and scratch it'. As the Ranks' history already quoted writes: 'the quality of life for the majority of the population improved beyond recognition. People were healthier and better fed than ever before. Medical treatment, available to all, pushed infantile mortality down to an all time low level.' The Rowntree Survey supports this. Whereas in 1946 thirty-one per cent of working-class families were living in poverty, by 1951 the figure had dropped dramatically to 2.8 per cent. In Sheffield the infantile mortality rate had nearly halved and for the first time ever was similar to the figure for the rest of England and Wales, whereas at the end of the First World War it had been twenty-five per cent higher than in the remainder of the country. Due to the unprecedented demand caused by war-time destruction unemployment in the immediate post-war period was lower than ever before. In every year but one from 1921 to 1939 ten per cent of the insured population had been unemployed; now in the post-war period unemployment had virtually disappeared. In fact another new term was coined to describe the situation: 'overfull employment'. This laid the basis for the Welfare State and gave the trade union movement the opportunity of winning increased wages and a shorter working week.

All this led to a change in the type of food eaten, shifting from the fillers like bread to 'T' bone steaks. Wheat was consumed in other forms, such as breakfast cereals, and now, for the first time, obesity was becoming a problem for the ordinary people. This led to the making of the slimming loaf.

VI Claywheels Lane – Seventh Bakery

This was a very different situation from the one which George Fletcher and his father had faced following the First World War. The Penistone Road bakery, as a result of excessive overwork during the war years, was now practically worn out. George knew, for reasons explained earlier, that it could never be made to house the type of bakery now emerging in the new technological age, so the search was on for a new, much bigger site. One such site was investigated in the Sheffield suburb of Handsworth which lies on the south-eastern side of the city. It proved unsuitable. And as often happens to people wrestling with difficult problems, the solution emerged at a most unexpected moment.

One winter's evening George along with his son Paul, now aged ten, who had returned a war-time evacuee from Leverton, were sledging with Bert Slack down Batchelors Hill at Wadsley Bridge. Viewing the expanse of level ground before him George saw the possibilities of the Claywheels Lane site. It came as a revelation! Next day George Fletcher contacted his accountant who arranged for the three-acre site to be inspected along with the architect. George had always consulted his father when decisions of great moment had to be taken, and so now he arranged for his father to be present. A viewing party of four went out to inspect the green field site. 'My God,' said George Henry, 'what a wonderful bakery we could put up here. Who owns the land?' he asked. 'The Duke of Norfolk,' replied the architect. Whereupon George Henry, conscious of his political reputation, remarked: 'We will never get it.' But he was wrong! They did, first renting the land, and buying it in 1977.

The decision to build the plant at Claywheels Lane, undoubtedly the most momentous one in George Fletcher's life, was a

Claywheels Lane: George Fletcher's dream come true

gamble in which he sank not only all the earnings of the bakeries, but also a sizeable loan from the banks. Not surprisingly the banks had no inhibitions in loaning the money, which was quickly repaid. They knew that Fletchers were a good risk, having built up a business from scratch and living anything but the lives of luxury. The first sod was cut shortly after the site was acquired in July 1945. It was five years before the first loaf was baked in May 1950. Between those two notable dates there were many heartaches caused by the war-time shortages and the great demands on building materials and labour for reconstruction. They all made the job of building the new plant a veritable nightmare. Yet there was no one more fitted than 'young George' – as he was known – to face and overcome them. He was now in the prime of life with twenty years' experience, spurred on with the prospects of achieving his life's ambition. It has been well said that George Fletcher was his own 'clerk of works'.

The great day dawned for George Fletcher when Stan Jackson, shift foreman, and ten men, in the presence of Bert Slack poured flour, salt, lard and water into the mixing machines and set in motion the process of baking the first loaves at Claywheels Lane.

Forty-five minutes later the first batch of golden crispy bread emerged from the six-sack 'Uniflow' oven and was greeted with smiles of satisfaction from all who had made it possible. None more so than George Fletcher. Yet there was no time to start the corks popping from the champagne bottles! Much remained to be done and many problems to be solved before the celebrations could start. Within a fortnight the second shift of bakers was started, to be followed a few months later by the third shift. Another twelve months were to elapse before the cooling plant from Penistone Road was installed, which enabled the bread to be sliced and wrapped.

Come 1952 a second six-sack 'Uniflow' was installed. Each oven was capable of producing 1400 one and three-quarter pound loaves each hour, nearly three times the output of the speeded-up travelling oven at Penistone Road. At Claywheels Lane there was sufficient capacity to meet all the demands for bread throughout the week plus the extra needed at weekends and at holiday times. With the transfer of bread production to Claywheels Lane Penistone Road bread production was shut down.

By now the number of shops supplied had risen from eight hundred in 1948 to over a thousand. The area covered extended beyond the suburbs of the city, taking in the smaller urban centres and villages.

It was another two years before confectionery production was transferred to Claywheels Lane in September 1954. Much of the confectionery at Penistone Road was done by hand. There were some machines in the pre-war days; the custards, for which Fletchers had a reputation, were made at the rate of twenty-eight per minute. Teacakes were rolled out three times as fast – eighty per minute. There were mixing machines and another one which rolled out the pastry. The cases for lemon and jam tarts, which in those days were in great demand, were also stamped out. Nevertheless rolling pins, unlike the ones found in the housewife's kitchen and so well loved by the music hall comics, were formidable weapons. They were three feet long and made of mahogany. Most of the women could not lift them.

In the early days at Penistone Road there were only eight women employed in making confectionery. Shortly after the department's transfer to Claywheels Lane the numbers had grown to sixty full-time staff working days and nights. There were also twenty-two women working part-time. In order to keep the place spotlessly clean, and in particular to get rid of the dirt caused by building operations, cleaners were introduced for the first time. Ever since they have remained amongst the most important section of all the staff employed.

Paul Fletcher Starts Work

At this stage it is necessary to break off the narrative to deal with two events, one happy, the other sad, which took place in the Fletcher establishment. In 1957 the third generation of the Fletcher family entered the business at Claywheels Lane. George Paul Fletcher, the son of George and Alice Fletcher, and known to everybody, workpeople and management alike, as Paul, started work at the age of twenty-two. In the same year he was also made a director, as was his mother. His upbringing had been very different from that of his grandfather and father. Nevertheless, as subsequent pages of this history will reveal, he was not to lose his common touch, nor be spared from the hard knocks of an industry so very different from the one experienced by his grandfather and father in their early days.

At the outbreak of the 1939 war he had been evacuated from the front-line city of Sheffield, spending the next five years with his grandparents at Leverton. There he attended the ordinary state South Leverton school. In 1944 when the Hitler armies were on the retreat he returned to Sheffield and became a pupil for two years at Oakwood School. Following this he enjoyed the happiest years of his school life at the Kings Moor Boarding School at Glossop. From there he became a student at the Manchester College of Technology, receiving instructions in all sides of the baking and confectionery industry under the expert tuition of Mr Albert R. Daniels, acknowledged as one of the most competent figures in the profession. He proved an apt pupil, gaining the City and Guild qualifications, following which he was called up and served two years in the RAF as a cook.

'I started work in 1957. This was also the year of my first marriage,' recalls Paul Fletcher; 'I was my father's assistant, taking some of the load off him. Over the years I have introduced new ideas.' Describing his early impressions of the bakery he said: 'I

Paul Fletcher (standing): his father's assistant

saw that everybody worked hard, but nobody was able to get a comprehensive view of what we were doing. So I introduced charts which showed how the output was faring.'

But to no one were these charts of greater importance than to Paul himself. The battle for trade was hotting up. Survival for long-established firms with modern plant was in the balance. More of this later.

George Henry's Death

The other event which marked these years was the death of George Henry Fletcher on 8th June 1958 at the age of seventy-nine years. It came a few months after the diamond wedding celebrating his marriage to Kate. His death was mourned by all who knew him, businessmen and workmen alike. His business associates regarded him with a respect seldom met with in a world where the touchstone of success was the size of the bank balance; his workpeople had an affection for him rarely accorded to the boss. These sentiments from both sides of industry are well summed up in the *Sheffield Telegraph* headline commenting on his death: 'Genial Communist who became a Capitalist'.

Outside the family none felt his loss more than the humble folk of Sheffield. He had shared their lot and fought with a selfless determination their battles of poverty and social deprivation. The greatest honour ever bestowed on him, which he treasured more than all the distinctions of the 'Honours List', was the presentation by the Bakers' Union of a free membership card and a certificate which reads:

> *In your day and generation you have done something to leave the world better than you found it.*

His wife Kate survived him for another nine years.

Men and women die, but what they have done lives on. It certainly did at Fletchers, for though the plant at Claywheels Lane is poles apart from the backstreet slum bakehouse at Kirk Street – which George Henry described as a 'Tin Pot affair' – the spirit which was a vital part of George Henry's character found its way into every Fletcher enterprise, and burns as brightly today as ever

Presentation of Bakers' Union free-membership card and certificate to George Henry Fletcher

One of the modern bread vans

it did. This is, in a word, his humanity – his compassion for his fellow men and women. To his customers it was expressed in the quality of his product. His workpeople he treated as equals, always concerned with their welfare. 'Are tha' all right lass?' was a constant enquiry he made as he moved amongst those who worked at his bakehouse.

Fierce Competition

Return we must to the bakehouse at Claywheels Lane which was very different from Penistone Road. By 1959 output of bread and confectionery was beginning to forge ahead at a remarkable pace. A quarter of a million loaves were being produced each week, nearly double the output at Penistone Road. Two hundred thousand units of confectionery, three varieties of tarts – jam, lemon and curd – chocolate gâteaux, and buns were being produced. To these must be added a hundred thousand items of morning goods, teacakes, bread rolls and other non-bread products intended for consumption on the day of production – in all a hundred times more than those produced at Penistone Road.

It required forty larger vans to distribute this growing quantity of bread and delectable fancy goods to the two thousand shops situated within a twenty-five mile radius of Sheffield. The staff now numbered 260. Yet the bakery was again confronted with serious problems. By the late 1950s the industry was moving into its most critical phase: big changes in ownership, marketing and technology were now forging ahead at an increasing speed. This must be seen against the background of a serious decline in total bread consumption in Britain. 'Demand had dropped by sixty-six per cent since the 1950s,' as John Silkin, Minister of Agriculture, Fisheries and Food, told the House of Commons on 10th April 1978. The *British Baker*, 14th April 1978, put the decline since 1956 at forty-six per cent, or in the graphic words of the *Sunday Times*, 23rd April 1978, 'Then [i.e. in the 1950s] people ate an average of two loaves a week. Now they eat only one.'

By takeovers, the 'Big Three' had acquired many new bakeries and retail outlets, including exclusive trading agreements with some of the increasingly important supermarkets. They repeatedly tried to get Fletchers. 'At least once a year they have tried to take us over,' George Fletcher has said. In the ten years ending 1975, the 'Big Three's' share of the declining market has increased by ten per cent. They now supply 61.5 per cent of ordinary bread consumption, achieving this dominating position by shutting down many of the bakeries they had acquired and building new ones based on the latest advances in baking technology. In the fourteen years ending 1972 the number of bakeries in the United Kingdom had been reduced by sixty-three per cent. Since then closures have continued apace. Spillers closed twenty-eight bakeries; Ranks Hovis MacDougall, thirty-two; Associated British Foods, eight. (*British Baker*, 14th April 1978).

Yet the most spectacular has occurred with the collapse in April 1978 of bread production at Spillers, when twenty-three plants were closed immediately and a cloud of uncertainty remains hanging over the thirteen incorporated into the remaining 'Big Two'. It was the decision of Tesco to drop Spillers French as a bread supplier at its seven hundred supermarkets which delivered the coup de grâce. Nevertheless it was not unwelcome to the remaining 'Big Two'; *British Baker*, already quoted, described it as a 'shot in the arm' to them.

The spur which drove this development ruthlessly forward was the need to keep afloat in what was now a fiercely competitive industry. It produced two complementary results. Firstly there were more bread-making plants in Britain than there were mouths willing to eat the bread. It is difficult to quantify this because of the unevenness of demand. Twenty-five per cent of all bread sold is bought on Saturdays; to retain its freshness it is essential that it should not have left the oven more than twenty-four hours earlier. The consequence is that at weekends and holidays much of the idle plant is brought into full production. This should be borne in mind when it is noted that around thirty per cent of bread making in the bakeries owned by the 'Big Three' is working at less than ninety per cent of capacity. Nevertheless it is accepted that there is 'a significant amount of spare, excess, underutilised . . . bread-making plant'. (*Monopolies Commission Report*, Par. 290.) With the demise of bread baking at Spillers Mr Michael Vernon, the Chairman, said that 'the company's withdrawal from baking bread would reduce the industry's over-capacity from about ten per cent to two per cent.' (*Guardian*, 8th April 1978.) However, 'the Federation of Bakers puts it at about twenty per cent.' (*British Baker*, 14th April 1978.)

Then, confronted with excess capacity there started in the early sixties what has been described in battlefield language as the 'discount war', which increased in intensity up to 1975, reaching 'up to thirty-five per cent off retail list prices . . . to some customers. . . .' (Monopolies Commission Report, Par. 484.) Mr Arthur Hughes, Assistant General Secretary of the United Road Transport Union, claims that discounts are between forty to fifty per cent. (*British Baker*, 14th April 1978.)

Technological Changes

The changes in the technology of baking were equally important. The new and modernised plants being installed in this period incorporated advances in both the method of preparing the dough (known as the Chorleywood Bread Process) and baking it. The new method of dough preparation reduced the amount of time necessary to prepare the dough ready for putting into the prover from three hours to under fifteen minutes, eliminating bowl fermentation. At the same time it increased the number of loaves per sack by four per cent. The new type of oven 'reduced the baking time by one quarter' (Augustus Muir, *The History of Baker Perkins*, p. 149.) It also reduced the amount of crust, producing the modern soft eating bread which when wrapped keeps much longer than crusty bread. There are those who are very critical of this type of loaf, claiming it is much inferior to the crusty loaf. Yet if purchases are the yardstick the housewife prefers the soft eating type. A survey carried out by Ranks Hovis MacDougal in 1965 showed that three out of every four housewives had bought this type of bread in the previous weeks. Even the French people, who are renowned for their crusty 'baguette' which they purchase three times a day, are now going over to this type of bread.

Confronted with this situation Fletchers had to take urgent action or else they would get on the slippery slope of decline, leading to 'takeover' or bankruptcy – a fate which has engulfed so many long-established family concerns throughout the country and has at last caught the baking section of one of the 'Big Three'. In the Sheffield area names like Davys, Brooms, Gillotts, Styans, Newbould and Veres are but memories whose glories lie in the past. Though in some cases trading under these names still continues, they are no longer family establishments. One such example is Gunstones whose founder was William Gunstone. He started the business as a grocery shop in 1862 – 116 years ago – progressing to food manufacture and bread baking over a number of years. Now they are owned by Northern Foods Limited, making morning goods but not bread.

Fletchers' first, and in Paul Fletcher's opinion, most important decision was to scrap their 'Uniflow' ovens, replacing them by the new type known as the 'turbo-radiant'. The first was installed in 1963. 'We were quite happy with the crusty bread,' said Mr Slack, the manager; 'it was very good eating bread but the housewife didn't want it.' 'Within twelve months of installing the new plant we doubled our sales of sliced bread,' recalls Paul Fletcher, Managing Director. 'Before that,' he continues, 'our trade was static, even declining. We were financially sound, but without trade, finances rapidly dwindle away.'

Today the plant produces four hundred thousand loaves of bread a week, in sixteen different lines, as against two hundred and fifty thousand in 1950. And in line with their past record the quality of the new loaf is unequalled, having won in 1965, for the third

Turbo-radiant oven

time, a trophy for the best plant bread produced. 'It is not a question of profit,' continues Paul Fletcher,

> 'we make more profit on crusty bread. The customer only pays half a pence more for the plain standard large loaf sliced and wrapped yet it costs us three-quarters of a pence for the bag alone, on top of which must be added the wages of those operating the slicing and bagging machines, plus the waste resulting from the bagging machines. These often malfunction, causing us more headaches than any other piece of machinery in the bakery.'

Today whilst other costs have increased, the bagging operation is responsible for putting two-pence on a loaf, the price of which since 1960 has gone up from twelve old pence to twenty-eight new pence today.

Of course entry into the Common Market has also increased the price of flour, which *The Times* described as due to 'punitive levies

. . . imposed on . . . milling wheat from North America,' from which the best flour is milled. This has resulted in lower grades being used in ordinary bread, which is one reason for bread not being what it used to be. However Fletchers' flour contains ten to fifteen per cent more Canadian wheat than the flour normally used by the Chorleywood process of bread making. This is one of the reasons for their better quality bread.

The decision to instal the second 'turbo-radiant' was taken in 1968. Based on George Fletcher's experience with the first, he had devised forty-two modifications which he insisted must be incorporated into the second oven. 'Every one of them was good' said Baker Perkin's representative:

> 'He wanted a plant identical with the one already installed which though it is not in production all the time acts as a standby and allows for thorough maintenance. In my opinion Fletchers is the best maintained bakery I know. You see most bakeries are in a shocking state because they try to run the plant all the time. Not so Fletchers, they have two plants.'

Fletchers had not the trade to justify the second 'turbo-radiant'. The first alongside the old 'uniflow' was quite adequate. 'But the old oven looked so antiquated and was so labour intensive that I urged it should be replaced by a second 'turbo-radiant'. Some people thought we were mad,' recalled Paul Fletcher:

> "They urged us to leave the money in the bank where it would earn more money in interest than it did, at that time, as plant. But a new plant enabled us to improve the organisation and appearance of the bakehouse. Now in the recent period it has proved a real boon and its monetary value has appreciated many more times.'

Early in 1970 the high-speed mixing and rapid fermentation were introduced.

During the 1950s a new retailing technique, known as the mobile shop, made its appearance. It was a response to the 'Big Three' in order to break into each other's exclusively controlled retail trade, and to take advantage of the rehousing of the population on the new housing estates, where it was more difficult to buy the odd loaf from a nearby house window shop. Fletchers themselves, feeling the pinch, decided to follow suit. It was Paul, with his eye on his charts, who urged that they should do this. The mobile shops proved so successful that by the mid-sixties they had some fifty-six of them. In Sheffield – with the exception of Fletchers who still have forty – they have virtually disappeared. They were swept away by a combination of the supermarkets and the disappearance, with one or two exceptions, of the production by plant bakers of the traditional confectionery lines, without which mobile shops are difficult to sustain.

Confectionery

Open confectionery can be produced in an automated plant but for it to arrive on the table undamaged and fresh is a difficult operation which the large-plant bakers have abandoned in favour of the prepacked lines. Not so Fletchers! They are one of the largest fully automated producers of traditional confectionery in the north of England, but forever on the look-out for new lines without which the department would quickly go into decline. There are nine lines of machines all making different types of open confectionery, some

One of the fifty modern mobile shops

Made by George Fletcher, this enrobing machine is covering cakes with fondant

producing ten thousand units per hour. George Fletcher was the brain behind many of the extensive modifications to machines, which have replaced nearly all the hand production by much faster mechanical methods. He also designed a piece of apparatus which is quite unique. It is a twenty-two-station dispenser made of stainless steel which weighs out the ingredients. 'It's so professional,' said Don Gill, Baker Perkins' representative; 'many of his improvements have, in fact, been incorporated in our equipment.' He continued, 'I used to pull his leg by saying, the only thing he couldn't improve was his Rolls-Royce.'

Many of the old-fashioned best-sellers such as jam, lemon curd tarts, and custards have been toppled from the head of the charts by new lines, such as Devon Puffs and updated vanilla slices, which are produced at the rate of five thousand a day. There are two types of doughnuts and three thousand five hundred are made daily. A very recent innovation is the making of a line with the intriguing description of 'elephant's feet' – a type of chocolate éclair which in the first week sold five thousand a day. Of all the confectionery made within the last seven years one-third consists of new lines.

Though more time is spent in making today's best-selling lines, the number of different units produced in Fletcher's confectionery department is the same as with the more labour-intensive production of fifteen years ago. One of the factors responsible is the introduction of the high-speed mixing of the dough for the morning goods. This enabled the department to dispense with shift working: it opens at 6 am and closes at 5 pm employing ninety women and twenty-two men.

During this period – the mid 1960s – Fletchers launched out in a more conventional way into the retail trade by acquiring in addition to their first shop a permanent shop in the centre of Sheffield, to be followed shortly by the opening of another twelve in various parts of the city. They are under the control of Paul's second wife Gloria, whom he married in 1968. They are a success, and in the Fletcher tradition most of the premises are owned by the business.

At first Fletchers refused to supply supermarkets, a decision they reversed on the urging of Paul Fletcher. Now they produce

Fletchers' Exchange Street shop

one-fifth of Sheffield's bread and much of its confectionery.

Why Have Fletchers Survived?

Many have been puzzled as to why Fletchers have managed to survive. There are those who do not accept that there is not a private arrangement with one or other of the 'Big Three' – now the 'Big Two'. Others like Mr Eric Gunstone, one time President of the Bakers' Federation, have remarked 'how well they husbanded their resources'. The first explanation is not true; there is a great deal of truth in the second one! Yet the most apt explanation of all is that given by Mr Bert Slack, the retired bakery manager: 'Fletchers' success is due to the mental intellect of the Fletchers, the loyalty and skill of their work people.' So far in this history both factors have been dealt with, as have the great technical changes between Claywheels Lane and Penistone Road. Not so the labour relations of this period. Now is the time to make good that omission.

Throughout the years relations between the workforce and the Fletcher family have been described by the workpeople, trade-union officials and the press alike in the most glowing terms. This is to be expected with a man of George Henry Fletcher's calibre who led a life of public service dedicated to the interests of the ordinary people. Though neither his son nor his grandson Paul played a similar public role, their relations within the factory have been cast in a similar mould. The relationship is neither paternalistic nor of a master–servant type. Nor does nepotism exist, as was revealed when a member of the Fletcher family, employed in a managerial capacity, was prematurely retired for not doing his job properly and in consequence causing dissatisfaction amongst the workpeople. None of the employees believed it would ever happen, but it did. Over and over again all the sections of the bakery have likened the relationship to that of a family – a description I have used only after the most careful investigation. A typical example was the letter signed by the majority of those employed in the confectionery department and published in the Sheffield newspaper the *Morning Telegraph* on 20th October 1977. In part it read: 'perhaps we are lucky to have a boss in a million. We are not statistics on a profit and loss sheet. We are his employees in what is still a family business . . .'.

It may be thought that this is a view engineered by a clever management and canvassed by individuals anxious for promotion. No such motivation can be attributed to Mr Sam Maddox, militant General Secretary of the Food and Allied Workers Union. Following a visit in August 1977 to Fletchers' Bakery he wrote 'at this bakery I witnessed the most sound and stable industrial relations I have ever seen in my life.' (The *Bakery Worker*, October 1977.) It is a view re-echoed by Bill French, divisional organiser of the Road Transport Workers Union which organises the van men, who said, 'I always looked with much affection on George Fletcher.' Comparing negotiations at Fletchers with other bakeries: 'they were more satisfactory here . . .'. There can be few enterprises which have had similar tributes paid to them.

Following the two national strikes in September and November 1977 when it was Paul Fletcher who urged his workmen to stop work, the press were so amazed that they ran feature articles describing this strange phenomenon. One such article was published in the *Sheffield Star* 28th November 1977 under the byline, 'Fletchers' Secret Ingredient', which I have used as the title of this book.

Not all the workforce share this view, but indisputably it is the opinion of the great majority. This is not to say there are no differences which at times are sharp and strongly felt. But they are all resolved without strikes! The vast majority within the factory seldom invoke the disputes procedure or need the intervention of a full-time trade-union officer. It is best summed up by Dick Martin, shop steward for the van men, who have no inhibitions in saying exactly what they think. 'Yes,' he said; 'we are a family but like most families we have our rows. Sometimes they are more serious than others, but we get over them.' One other van man said, 'I've been "sent down the lane" by one of the directors who next day apologised for being so hasty.'

One such row was over what has become known as the 'haircut dispute'. It happened in March 1972. George Fletcher, always concerned with the personal appearance of his sales staff, insisted that the hair should not hang over the collar or the sideboards go under the chin and link up with the moustache. 'As a food firm we have to be very careful. We don't want our reputation ruined,' he told the *Morning Telegraph*. So he gave all those transgressing this ruling two days in which to get their hair cut. All but three complied. One of those, who at first refused, was a shop steward. He considered it 'an invasion of our personal freedom.' It seemed that the first ever strike was imminent. But it was not to be – though the trade-union full-time official was apprehensive at the prospect of a shop steward being sacked, after a mass meeting in the canteen between the management and men, everybody complied with the haircut rule.

Strange as it may seem, in the recent period there have been two short strikes both called at the insistence of management. The first was in 1974 following an arbitration wages award which the trade-union members throughout Britain would not accept. This resulted in the union calling the membership out on strike. The Fletchers' bakers did not want to join the strike because the issue in dispute did not affect them. Nevertheless Paul Fletcher had a meeting with his workpeople and insisted that if an official strike was called they had no alternative but to respond. However it was discovered that a Rotherham bakery had been given a dispensation by the union to work, which resulted in the Fletchers' bakers saying, 'if they work we do', and they did.

Happy pickets outside Fletchers

The other occasion was in August 1977. The union decided to insist that no bakery in Britain should work on bank holiday, or if they did, then payment should be made in lieu. Failure to get either of these demands satisfied resulted in the union calling their members out on strike, on 10th September 1977. Earlier in July the bakers' union had signed a separate agreement with Fletchers which the membership insisted exempted them from any nationally called strike. However, pickets appeared at the factory gates and were treated to sandwiches and cups of coffee, an unheard of gesture. As Fletchers were anxious to avoid a confrontation, Paul Fletcher decided that the bakery should stop work, but following a mass meeting of union members it was decided to resume work claiming their separate agreement excluded them from the national dispute.

The separate agreement which Fletchers have with the bakers' union is part of the industrial strategy of its managing director, Paul Fletcher. No one knows better than he that the bakery workers' wages are well down the league table, and in recent years the bakers' union has been pursuing more militant policies with the aim of ending this situation. If Fletchers could pay the average manufacturing wage and stay in business they would, but to keep alive in an industry so precariously balanced is a very difficult task. Therefore wages and conditions must bear some relationship to those prevailing within the industry. Nevertheless those employed at Fletchers are better off than their counterparts working in other bakery concerns. This is because Paul Fletcher, well informed of trade-union policies, and anxious to end the below average wages in the baking industry, but determined to keep his bakery alive, hit upon the idea of concluding a separate agreement with the unions. This agreement has given wage levels better than those prevailing in the rest of the industry and, vitally important, avoided the disruption which strikes cause. This approach has made a vital contribution to the Fletcher success story.

It is no exaggeration to say, therefore, that in Britain there is no establishment which has greater sympathy with the aims of the trade-union movement than Fletchers. Jack Davis, full-time official of the bakers' union, said: 'It was George Fletcher, a member of the Federation of Bakers, who played the main part in getting the one hundred per cent trade unionism clause incorporated into the agreement between the employers and the union.' And following in his father's footsteps, it was Paul who insisted on all their workers joining a union even when the Industrial Relations Act of 1972 made a 'closed shop' illegal. Trade-union contributions are stopped at source which entitles the firm to take a 5.5 per cent commission. Fletchers never take it; instead it is put into the union's benevolent fund.

Pensions, Profit-Sharing, Canteen

Sympathy with trade unionism, important as it is, need cost little. At Fletchers it costs a lot. The pension scheme introduced in 1937 was, in the late 1960s, converted into a non-contributory scheme, the firm paying nine per cent of every eligible full-time employee's wages into the pension fund. This now costs around £50,000 a year. After a qualifying period of three years the recipient is in full benefit, which in the event of death includes the payment of a year's salary to the next of kin.

Fletchers have the distinction of being one of the few firms in Britain who have a profit-sharing scheme. After tax twenty-five per cent of profits are shared out on a points system to all full-time employees. Some £143,908 has been paid out since it was introduced in 1969.

The canteen is unusual in two ways. Firstly it is subsidised, and in the seven years since 1971 it has cost the firm £94,054, providing a meal for approximately thirty pence. There are few bakeries who have anything similar. But to some, its most remarkable feature is its common feeding arrangements, well illustrated by the following George Fletcher incident. After showing a small group of business associates round the bakery he took them to the canteen. It was lunchtime. One of the party enquired: 'Where do we eat?', to which George replied, 'tha feeds here.' 'Oh, then there is only one canteen,' continued his questioner. 'Yes,' replied George; 'everybody sits at the same tables.' When George got to the serving counter he reached to his pocket for money. Nonplussed his visitor asked, 'And do we have to pay as well?' 'Yes or else tha goes hungry,' replied George.

One other aspect vital to Fletchers labour relations is the contact between the workforce and the directors. The latter do not sit in ivory towers remote from the shop floor. Both George, and today Paul, are constantly moving around the plant giving a helping hand when hitches occur. One maintenance fitter said to me, 'I have had Paul labouring for me.' But at the same time and most important of all, he is exercising strict quality control along with the production director, Mr Gordon Glover.

In writing about the labour–management relations at Fletchers I have tried not to overpaint the picture. Many more instances could have been recounted all of which may have resulted in presenting an unbelievably idyllic scene of near perfection. To do this would in my judgement have been wrong. There are those who are dissatisfied. This is mainly on the bakery side, where there is a twenty per cent turnover of labour, due mainly to the unsocial hours of shifts and the monotony of automated production, though there are those who leave for higher wages which can be earned *outside* the baking industry. Nevertheless within the limitations imposed through competition by other bakery enterprises Fletchers' labour relations are an example worthy of study by all interested in ending the upheavals which occur in some of Britain's industry.

Visitors: Housewives and Students

A feature of the bakery is the constant stream of visitors – bakery students and housewives – who regularly inspect the bakery. Mr Knowles, Sheffield's Chief Food Inspector – now retired – told me: 'as lecturer at the Sheffield College of Technology for Public Health Inspectors every twelve months I took my students to Fletchers.' The visits of housewives started in 1958 when the manager and George Fletcher started taking parties round during the early evening. The demand on the time of both men was so great that it had to be abandoned. It was restarted in 1972 by Mrs Gloria Fletcher. Four times a week groups of visitors are taken on conducted tours. The demand is so great that twelve months elapse between the request for a visit and its fulfilment. Hundreds of appreciative letters have been received praising not only what they have seen – especially its cleanliness – but also expressing gratitude for the products the visitors regularly purchase. One such complimentary letter from an eighty-one-year-old reads 'how pleasing to [be] served by one of your salesmen, who sir is a credit in the way

The annual dinner and dance, Phoenix Rooms, Rotherham 1970

he performs his duties and how clean he keeps his van, so appetising the products . . . and I must say excellent the quality . . .'. These visiting parties are of the greatest value to the firm, says Paul Fletcher: 'they enable the public to cast a critical eye over the making of our bread and confectionery which assists both the management and the workpeople to keep the hygiene in the bakery in tip-top condition.' A condition well appreciated by Mr Knowles, mentioned above, whose family ate Fletchers' bread: 'we knew what we were buying,' he told me.

Sports

The Fletcher story has to finish on both a happy and a sad note. Starting with the outbreak of the Second World War the word picture is one of gruelling long hours of unrelieved hard physical and mental labour. There are relaxations, the sports club provides entertainment to all those wanting to join. Fishing is the most popular.

Once a year there is the firm's dinner and dance, probably the most patronised of all these events. As for the Fletchers, they have

George Fletcher, Yorkshire's karting champion, 1963

established quite a reputation for their 'Karting' activities, which is the not so wealthy man's motor racing.

The sport was introduced to Britain by an American Airforce officer around 1959. George Fletcher, whose passion for things mechanical – especially motor cars – has been with him from his earliest days, constructed at the rear of the bakery, together with his son Paul, a primitive motor car obstacle race during which they 'screeched' old cars around posts which had been erected on the big concrete expanse. Around 1960 an enthusiast of the Doncaster Kart Club, hearing of this, got in touch with Paul enquiring if one Sunday they could bring the Karts to use the primitive track, a request to which they eagerly agreed. Both George and Paul had a go and found it so exhilarating that they decided to join in the real thing. From then their skill rapidly developed until both of them became champions – George the Yorkshire Champion in 1963, while Paul became a member of the British Kart racing team competing in forty international events – a record which has so far been unequalled. 'I finished third in the world championships one year,

Paul Fletcher, competitor in forty international karting events

second in the European championships another year. I was in the team which won the European championships outright,' Paul told me. He stopped international racing because it took up too much of his time, though he still races nearly every Sunday. 'I find the sport so absorbing that I haven't time to even think about the bakery until Monday morning.'

Death of George Fletcher

The sad event occurred on 18th September 1973, with the death of George Fletcher, at the age of sixty-nine years. It cast a gloom over the factory. Tributes poured in from all sides, from the President of the Bakers' Federation of which for many years he was an outstanding member – and would have been its president but for his politics – and from many of the baking enterprises in all parts of Britain. His wife Alice was filled with a despair which is impossible to describe in words. His contribution to the success story of Fletchers is beyond compare. He started life in humble circumstances endowed with a mechanical bent of genius and a determination to forge ahead no matter how great the difficulties.

These pages have shown that he won through. His memorial is

no plaque or statue, but a modern thriving bakery which he conceived and played the major part in building in an industry from which so many of his contemporaries have been ousted.

The New Managing Director

George was succeeded by his son Paul as managing director. Could he, a young fellow of thirty-seven, carry on the business? Many in the bakery world thought not. Now was the time to make even more tempting 'takeover bids'. But they have been proved wrong. If he does not have the mechanical bent of his father he has more business acumen. 'My father had a marvellous ability to shut out the world and concentrate on perfecting the machine,' says his son Paul. 'It was because he was such a good engineer that we succeeded at a time when technology was the key to advance. He was not only his own chief mechanic, but the production manager and the sales director.' Now these managerial posts are filled by highly efficient people all promoted from the shop floor, which leaves Paul Fletcher with an overall view of the bakery and, equally important, of what is happening in the world outside.

Two examples to illustrate this will suffice. A representative of Spillers French, now retired, who supplied Fletchers with some of their flour, told me that he was forever protesting to his employers at the high price they charged Fletchers, but was shut up. Paul Fletcher on reading this said 'By God! Nobody overcharges us for flour these days. What's more we continually "shop" around seeking out the cheapest sources of supply for all our requirements, providing of course it is the best.'

One innovation Paul has made is the installation of an independent power unit. This followed the power cuts in 1972. At the time when these first occurred the government department concerned had handed over to the top bakery concerns responsibility for allocating the limited power supplies. The result could have been to Fletchers' disadvantage. Determined to remain independent, Paul Fletcher installed a unit which can produce enough power to run both ovens, or one oven and the confectionery department. And what a boon it has turned out to be.

In 1976 a committee called the Consortium Committee was set up. It is made up of the four directors Paul and Gloria

Fletcher, Gordon Glover, production director, and Arnold Hill, sales director, plus two representatives from the bigger departments and one from the smaller ones. It meets four times a year. The managing director gives a résumé of events in the industry and informs them how the directors propose to deal with the situation; what new machinery it is planned to buy; and the new products they intend launching. He analyses the bakery's successes and failures. At the last two quarterly meetings Paul Fletcher warned them of the imminent collapse of Spiller-French and of Hawleys. Not often do these topics provoke much discussion, the domestic topics of the shop floor being preferred. Nevertheless the new committee has been welcomed by all the departments for it keeps them in touch with the issues vital to their continued employment.

Epilogue

There is little left for me to write by way of lessons. This history of the three generations of Fletchers speaks for itself.

The seven bakeries have been and are unique – from the first humble 'tinpot affair' which started in the Victorian slums of Sheffield's east end to the present-day modern bakery which lies behind magnificent gardens so pleasing to the eye.

When George Henry and his wife Kate started the first venture they did everything. They fetched the flour, mixed the dough, baked the bread, then sold it door to door and outside the factories. Even then George Henry found time with the early socialist pioneers to seek support from amongst his fellow men for his principles.

Today there is a team of five hundred men and women ranging from the managing director to the young school leaver co-operating successfully in operating this, the seventh, 'technological wonder', in a fiercely competitive world from which so many of their contemporaries have been eliminated. Many have asked, what is the secret? It can be summed up in two words. They cared! – for those who bought the Fletcher products and for those who made them. Long may it continue!

Index